N.

HarperCollins*Publishers*

This book was produced using QuarkXPress™ and
Adobe Illustrator 88™ on Apple Macintosh™ computers
and output to separated film on a Linotronic™ 300 Imagesetter

Text: Carolyn Donaldson
Images: Portfolios Photography
Cartography: Susan Harvey Design
Design: Ted Carden

First published 1991
Copyright © HarperCollins Publishers
Produced by Collins Manufacturing, Glasgow
ISBN 0 00 435752-3

HOW TO USE THIS BOOK

Your Collins Traveller Guide will help you find your way around your holiday destination quickly and easily. It is split into two sections which are colour-coded:

The blue section provides you with an alphabetical sequence of headings, from **BARS** to **WALKS** via **EXCURSIONS**, **RESTAURANTS**, **SHOPPING**, etc. Each entry within a topic includes information on how to get there, how much it will cost you, when it will be open and what to expect. Furthermore, every page has its own map showing the position of each item and the nearest landmark. This allows you to orientate yourself quickly and easily in your new surroundings.
To find what you want to do – having dinner, visiting a museum, going for a walk or shopping for gifts – simply flick through the blue headings and take your pick!

The red section is an alphabetical list of information. It provides essential facts about places and cultural items – 'What is the Glockenspiel?', 'When is the Opernfestspiele?', 'Where is Dachau?' – and expands on subjects touched on in the first half of the book. This section also contains practical travel information. It ranges through how to find accommodation, where to hire a car, the variety of eating places and food available, tips on health, information on money, which newspapers are available, how to find a taxi and where the youth hostels are. It is lively and informative and easy to use. Each band shows the first three letters of the first entry on the page. Simply flick through the bands till you find the entry you need!

All the main entries are also cross-referenced to help you find them. Names in small capitals – **CHILDREN** – tell you that there is more information about the item you are looking for under the topic on children in the first part of the book. So when you read 'see **CHILDREN**' you turn to the blue heading for **CHILDREN**. The instruction 'see **A-Z**', after a word, lets you know that the word has its own entry in the second part of the book. Similarly words in bold type – **Schwabing** – also let you know that there is an entry in the A-Z for the indicated name. In both cases you just look under the appropriate heading in the red section. Packed full of information and easy to use – you'll always know where you are with your Collins Traveller Guide!

INTRODUCTION

The German province of Bavaria and its capital, Munich, evoke a colourful picture of the quintessential Germany: hearty, prosperous, mature, cultured, and even provincial in a way which is all-too-often missing from our increasingly homogeneous European cities of today. And this picture of the city is one which has its basis firmly in reality, not just in travel agents' sales talk: despite its post-war industrialization, increasing traffic congestion and large foreign population, Munich has determinedly retained its provincial atmosphere, and this air still dominates its more cosmopolitan influences.

Yet there are many disparate elements in the picture which makes up Munich. This so-called 'secret capital of Germany' is one of the country's largest cities, an important manufacturing centre for precision instruments, electrical goods and various kinds of machinery and, perhaps more importantly for its many visitors, the country's true cultural centre: home to the Bavarian Film Studio, several prestigious museums, theatres and concert halls, and the wonderful new cultural centre at Gasteig.

Munich owes its establishment in 1158 to the opportunism of the Duke of Bavaria and Saxony, Henry the Lion. He destroyed a bridge which was owned by a local bishop over the River Isar at Föhring and built another bridge of his own upstream in order to charge tolls for crossing the river, thereby monopolizing the lucrative salt trade coming from Reichenhall. From these humble origins the village of Zu den Munichen rose to become a prosperous market town with its own mint. The legacy of these early mercantile days can still be seen in the predominance of butchers' shops around Peterskirche where meat stalls once stood, and at the Marienplatz, the old city's centre which was known merely as the Grain Market between the 14th and 19thC.

The great Wittelsbach family entered the Munich story a few years later in 1180 when the town was taken by one of its members who proclaimed himself Duke of Bavaria and founded a dynasty which reigned, with a few interruptions, until the end of World War I, when the last remaining member of the family died in exile in Hungary. Under the

Wittelsbachs' influence the city had steadily grown and flourished, reaching a peak in the 14thC when Duke Ludwig IV was German Emperor and Munich an imperial city. The last German Emperor to be crowned by the Pope, Ludwig was later excommunicated and the city subsequently became a centre for rationalism, dissent and anti-papal feeling, attracting thinkers like William of Ockham (after whom Occamstrasse is named). The death of the Emperor brought a period of decline but by the 15thC the burghers had achieved more power and wealth and the city underwent a period of fostering of the arts: beautiful Gothic buildings such as the Alte Rathaus (Old Town Hall) and the Frauenkirche were built; the painter Jan Pollack came from Poland to adorn the cathedral and the Peterskirche; and the sculptor Erasmus von Grasser created his famous *Morisk Dancers* which you can still see in the Stadtmuseum.

By the end of the 16thC Munich was at the centre of the Counter-Reformation in Germany: Protestants were persecuted, Lutheran tracts and teaching were banned, the Jesuit college, the Alte Academie, was established, and the Michaelskirche built. The Wittelsbachs continued to mark the city with their cultural stamp: Wilhelm IV established an art gallery in the first Hofgarten, commissioning painters to fill it, and his son laid the foundations of what was to become the extensive Bavarian State Library. The Thirty Years' War in the first half of the 17thC, however, drained the city's finances and the problem was exacerbated by the extravagance of Prince Elector Ferdinand Maria and his wife who modelled both the life of their court and their palaces at Nymphenburg on the excesses of the French court at Versailles. It is to this period that the work of luminaries such as Joseph Effner, the Asam brothers, Cuvilliés and Johann Baptist Straub belongs, and their splendid late-baroque and rococo buildings are probably some of the finest you can see in the city today. Modern-day Munich's beauty seems all the more remarkable when one remembers that the city suffered extensive damage from bombing raids in the last war. Many of the buildings were subsequently restored to their former glory, and the splendour of the city's past and its history have successfully been retained.

One of Munich's main attractions as a holiday destination is the ease with which the visitor can experience the natural beauty of the rolling

Bavarian uplands, a pleasant complement to the bustle of the city, the man-made grandeur of its buildings and the exhausting conviviality of its nightlife. This was where the dreamy Ludwig II, another Wittelsbach and the patron of Richard Wagner, built the romantic, fairy-tale castles which have become so associated with the Bavarian landscape. The castles tend to be situated in beautiful positions overlooking the lovely Bavarian lakes where you can generally participate in all types of water sport. If you are the active type you will find that hiking in Bavaria or taking a trip down the river in a raft is a delightful way to experience the countryside at first-hand, while ascending by cable car or mountain train to the summit of one of the nearest peaks, such as the Zugspitze, should not be missed. The region is also famous for its winter sports, while the city itself has the good fortune to possess superb Olympic-standard facilities dating from 1972 when it hosted the Games.

It is one of the city's oldest and most famous industries, brewing, which supplies the final tint in the colour of the Munich picture. The true importance of the role of beer in the life of the populace is exemplified

by the traditional annual spring tasting of the new brew at the Hofbräuhaus, the best-known of the city's beer gardens, when even the Bavarian parliament stops its session to allow members to attend to this vital matter. The biggest event in the city's calendar is that of the world-renowned Oktoberfest, a two-week orgy of beer drinking which attracts some seven million visitors every year. If you can't make it in October, don't worry, as this is not the only beer-orientated celebration held here: there are also the Starkbierfest (Strong Beer Festival) in winter and Fasching (Carnival) in spring, to name but two more. It is strange to

think that until the Middle Ages wine was the Bavarian tipple (and you can still taste some fine ones here), as even the hearty and nourishing Bavarian 'cuisine' seems designed particularly to accompany the local beers and lagers: thick soups, strongly flavoured sausages and sauerkraut! This heartiness is itself echoed in the character of and welcome offered by the good burghers to the many foreign visitors who flock to their beer cellars and beer gardens.

Whichever part of the picture of Munich and its surrounding country-side interests you most – architecture, art, festivals, history, theatres, sports venues, scenery or even just the beer – the combination of all its elements will beguile you into a lasting fondness for this city and its unique character.

Tegernsee

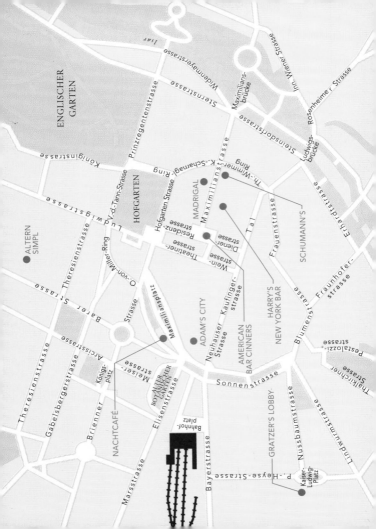

SCHUMANN'S Maximilianstrasse 36.
❑ 1700-0300 Sun.-Fri. Tram 19, 29.
Enjoys a chic cocktail-party atmosphere. The owner is a well-known Munich socialite.

MADRIGAL Herzog-Rudolf-Strasse 1.
❑ 1130-1400, 1800-0200. Tram 19, 29.
Always busy and frequented by celebrities. There is a bistro upstairs, a piano bar downstairs and a telefax machine which provides the latest stock-market reports.

HARRY'S NEW YORK BAR Falkenturmstrasse 9.
❑ 1600-0300 Mon.-Sat. U-Bahn 3, 6; S-Bahn Marienplatz.
Cosy bar offering a wide variety of drinks and especially well-known for its creative cocktails. Also a haunt of celebrities. Piano bar downstairs.

ALTERN SIMPL Türkenstrasse 57.
❑ 2100-0300. Mon.-Sat. U-Bahn 3, 6 Universität.
Famous Schwabing (see A-Z) literary café now frequented by political and show-biz personalities. Good atmosphere, but often packed.

NACHTCAFÉ Maximiliansplatz 5.
❑ 2100-0500. U-Bahn 4, 5; S-Bahn Karlsplatz.
Mixture of café, bar and music venue for yuppies with the right 'look'.

GRATZER'S LOBBY Beethovenplatz 2/3.
❑ 1700-0100 Mon.-Fri. (private parties Sat.). U-Bahn 3, 6 Goetheplatz.
Well-stocked bar serving gourmet snacks.

ADAM'S CITY Pacellistrasse 2.
❑ 0900-0700 (22 hr). U-Bahn 4, 5; S-Bahn Karlsplatz.
The place to go when everywhere else is shut (kitchen open till 0600!).

AMERICAN BAR CINNERS Residenzstrasse 3.
❑ 1100-0400. U-Bahn 3, 6; S-Bahn Marienplatz. Entrance in Hofgraben.
Light, modern decor and a young clientele.

HOFBRÄUHAUS Am Platzl 9.
❑ 0900-2400. U-Bahn 3, 6; S-Bahn Marienplatz.
The most famous beer hall of all! Try the noisy downstairs Schwemme
(tap room) with its band. Quieter upstairs room for groups. See **WALK 2**.

MATHÄSER BIERSTADT Bayerstrasse 7.
❑ 0800-2330. U-Bahn 4, 5; S-Bahn Karlsplatz.
*The biggest beer hall in the world, with 16 rooms and the capacity to
seat 5000 people. Attractions include a courtyard and live music.*

AUGUSTINERBRÄU Neuhauser Strasse 16.
❑ 0900-2400. U-Bahn 4, 5; S-Bahn Karlsplatz.
*Large restaurant and beer hall serving one of Munich's favourite and
oldest brews. Features a glass-domed 'grotto' and an attractive courtyard.*

AUGUSTINERKELLER Arnulfstrasse 52.
❑ 1130-2400. S-Bahn Hackerbrücke.
Particularly popular spot in summer because of its large beer garden.

HOFBRÄUKELLER Innere Wiener Strasse 19.
❑ 0800-2400. Tram 18.
*Spacious, typically Bavarian restaurant and beer hall situated in the
attractive district of Haidhausen. Large garden to the rear.*

SALVATOR-KELLER Am Nockherberg.
❑ 0900-2400. Tram 24, 27.
Typical beer hall with big garden. Venue of the Starkbierfest (see **Events**).

LÖWENBRÄUKELLER Nymphenburger Strasse 2.
❑ 0900-0100. U-Bahn 1 Stiglmaierplatz.
*Striking building with a distinctive tower, many different rooms, banquet-
ing hall, pleasant courtyard. Location of Fasching parties (see* **Events**).

DONISL Weinstrasse 1.
❑ 0800-0030. U-Bahn 3, 6; S-Bahn Marienplatz.
Balconied restaurant and beer hall with a long tradition. Live music.

RESIDENZ Max-Joseph-Platz 3.
U-Bahn 3-6 Odeonsplatz; S-Bahn Marienplatz.
Huge complex of buildings, home to generations of Bavarian nobility;
now houses the Residenzmuseum (see MUSEUMS 2). See WALK 3, A-Z.

ALTER HOF Burgstrasse 8.
❑ No admittance. U-Bahn 3, 6; S-Bahn Marienplatz.
The original residence of the Bavarian dukes before they moved to the
Residenz (see above). Today it houses a revenue office. See WALK 2, A-Z.

SCHLOSS NYMPHENBURG 8 km northwest of city centre.
❑ 0900-1230, 1330-1700 Tue.-Sat. (summer), 1000-1230, 1330-1600
(winter). Tram 12; bus 41. ❑ DM 5, Schloss only DM 2.50.
Summer palace of the electors of Bavaria. See NYMPHENBURG, A-Z.

SCHLOSS BLUTENBURG Obermenzing.
❑ Courtyard & church 0800-dusk. Bus 73, 76 from S-Bahn Pasing.
Former hunting palace of the Bavarian dukes. See A-Z, Children.

HAUPTPOST (PALAIS TÖRRING-JETTENBACH)
Residenzstrasse 2. U-Bahn 3, 6; S-Bahn Marienplatz.
Once owned by a count, now the Main Post Office. See WALK 3, A-Z.

PALAIS PORTIA Kardinal-Faulhaber-Strasse 12.
U-Bahn 3-6 Odeonsplatz; S-Bahn Marienplatz; tram 19.
Munich's first palace (1694) modelled on a baroque palazzo, then
remodelled in rococo by Cuvilliés (see A-Z). Now a bank. See WALK 3.

PREYSING-PALAIS Residenzstrasse 27.
U-Bahn 3-6 Odeonsplatz. Near the Feldherrnhalle.
First rococo palace in Munich, built by Joseph Effner (see A-Z) 1724-28.

ERZBISCHÖFLICHES PALAIS (ARCHBISHOPS' PALACE,
FORMERLY PALAIS HOLNSTEIN) Kardinal-Faulhaber-Strasse 7.
U-Bahn 3-6 Odeonsplatz; S-Bahn Marienplatz; tram 19.
Built for Prince Elector Karl Albrecht's son by Cuvilliés (see A-Z).

ALTES RATHAUS (OLD TOWN HALL) Marienplatz 15.
U-Bahn 3, 6; S-Bahn Marienplatz.
Germany's finest example of Gothic architecture. See **WALKS 1 & 2**, **A-Z**.

NEUES RATHAUS (NEW TOWN HALL) Marienplatz 8.
❑ Tower: 0900-1900 Mon.-Fri., 1000-1900 Sat., Sun., hol.
U-Bahn 3, 6; S-Bahn Marienplatz. ❑ DM 2.
An imposing neo-Gothic building housing the famous Glockenspiel (see **A-Z***) in its 85-m-high tower. See* **WALK 1**, **A-Z**.

HAUPTMÜNZAMT Hofgraben 4.
❑ 0800-1615 Mon.-Fri. U-Bahn 3, 6; S-Bahn Marienplatz.
The earliest example of Italian Renaissance architecture in the city. First served as the court stables and then the Mint. See **WALK 2**, **A-Z**.

MAXIMILIANEUM Max-Planck-Strasse 1.
❑ Apply at porter's lodge. U-Bahn 4, 5 Max-Weber-Platz; tram 19, 20.
Royal foundation originally providing free education. Still accommodates exceptional students and the Bavarian Parliament. See **WALK 2**, **A-Z**.

FELDHERRNHALLE Odeonsplatz. U-Bahn 3-6 Odeonsplatz.
A majestic copy of Florence's Loggia dei Lanzi, housing two bronze statues of the famous generals Tilly and Wrede. See **WALK 3**, **A-Z**.

ASAMHAUS Sendlinger Strasse 61.
U-Bahn 1-3, 6 Sendlinger Tor; S-Bahn Marienplatz.
18thC baroque house featuring a marvellously ornate facade. See **A-Z**.

LENBACHHAUS Luisenstrasse 33.
U-Bahn 2 Königsplatz.
Elegant Florentine-style villa, former Munich residence of artist Franz von Lenbach and now an art gallery (see **MUSEUMS 1***). See* **WALK 3**, **A-Z**.

PROPYLÄEN Königsplatz.
U-Bahn 2 Königsplatz.
Fine 19thC portico modelled on gateway to the Acropolis. See **WALK 3**.

LUITPOLD GRILL Brienner Strasse 11.
❑ 0900-2000 Mon.-Sat. U-Bahn 3-6 Odeonsplatz.
Legendary literary café (now also a restaurant) with an elegant clientele. Try one of the excellent cakes baked in their own shop.

GLOCKENSPIEL Marienplatz 2/V.
❑ 1000-2000. U-Bahn 3, 6; S-Bahn Marienplatz. Entrance in passage behind Schuh-Klein.
*Delightful spot overlooking carillon and Marienplatz (see **WALK 1**, **A-Z**).*

ARZMILLER Salvatorstrasse 2.
❑ 0830-1830. U-Bahn 3-6 Odeonsplatz. In the Theatinerhof.
Attractive café with a charming courtyard and an unusual fountain.

BODO'S BACKSTUBE Herzog-Wilhelm-Strasse 29.
❑ 0700-2100 (from 1000 Sun.). U-Bahn 1-3, 6 Sendlinger Tor.
Pleasant café owned by a well-known Munich personality.

CAFÉ RESIDENZ Sonnenstrasse 11.
❑ 0700-1900. U-Bahn 4, 5; S-Bahn Karlsplatz.
Spacious café with a gracious, old-fashioned atmosphere.

CAFÉ ANNAST Odeonsplatz 18.
❑ 0900-0100. U-Bahn 3-6 Odeonsplatz.
*Small café with plenty of tables set outside on the square and in the delightfully shady Hofgarten (see **PARKS & GARDENS**).*

ZUR SCHÖNEN MÜNCHERIN Karl-Scharnagl-Ring 60.
❑ 0900-1900 (from 1000 Sun.). Bus 53, 55.
*Stop here after a walk in the Englischer Garten (see **A-Z**). It's hung with copies of Ludwig I's Gallery of Beauties (see **Schloss Nymphenburg**).*

JOHANNIS Johannisplatz 15.
❑ 1100-0100 Mon., Wed., Thu., Sun., 1100-0300 Fri., Sat.
U-Bahn 4, 5 Max-Weber-Platz.
Traditional café with a difference – it's open at night. Mixed crowd.

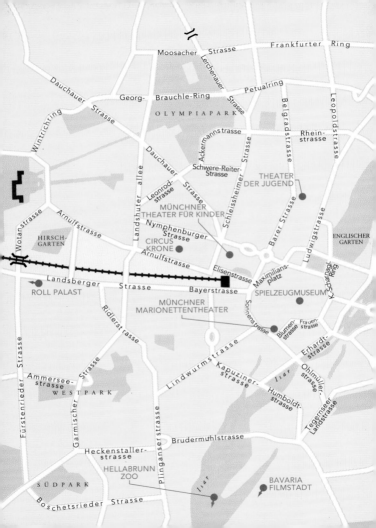

HELLABRUNN ZOO Siebenbrunner Strasse 6.
❏ 0800-1800 summer, 0900-1700 winter. U-Bahn 3 Thalkirchen.
6 km south of city centre. ❏ DM 5, child DM 3.
Europe's largest zoo with over 4500 animals living in geographic areas; specializes in breeding threatened species. Extensive children's corner.

THEATER DER JUGEND Franz-Joseph-Strasse 47.
❏ Bookings: 1330-1730 Tue.-Sat. Tram 18.
Modern plays in German, as well as mime for a variety of ages.

MÜNCHNER THEATER FÜR KINDER Dachauer Strasse 46.
❏ Bookings: 1000-1730 Mon.-Sat. U-Bahn 1 Stiglmaierplatz.
Mixture of plays including traditional fairy tales in German.

MÜNCHNER MARIONETTENTHEATER Blumenstrasse 29a.
❏ Bookings: 1000-1200 Tue.-Sun. (up to 1 hr before performance).
U-Bahn 1-3, 6 Sendlinger Tor.
Puppet theatre featuring performances of fairy tales in German (at 1500).

SPIELZEUGMUSEUM Altes Rathaus Turm, Burgstrasse 1.
❏ 1000-1730 Mon.-Sat., 1000-1800 Sun., hol. U-Bahn 3, 6;
S-Bahn Marienplatz. ❏ DM 3.
Descend the staircase through displays of toys from throughout the ages.

CIRCUS KRONE Marsstrasse 43.
❏ End Dec.-end March. S-Bahn Hackerbrücke.
A traditional circus, promising fun for all the family.

ROLL PALAST Aubinger Strasse 48.
❏ 1530-1830 Mon.-Thu., 1430-1830 Fri.-Sun. S-Bahn Westkreuz.
❏ DM 5, school hol. DM 4, skate hire DM 4.
Roller-skating rink with disco music, especially popular with teenagers.

BAVARIA FILMSTADT Bavaria-Film-Platz 7, Geiselgasteig.
❏ 0900-1600 1 Mar.-31 Oct. Tram 25. ❏ DM 10, child DM 6.
90-min tours by miniature train visiting the sets of famous German films.

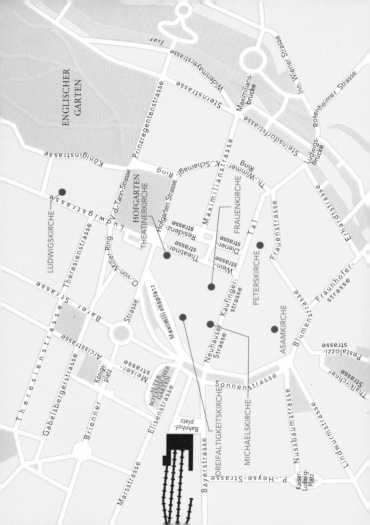

FRAUENKIRCHE (CHURCH OF OUR LADY) Frauenplatz 1.
U-Bahn 3, 6; S-Bahn Marienplatz. Beside the Feldherrnhalle.
The solemn late-Gothic brick exterior of Munich's cathedral hides a simple white interior, the result of impressive post-war restorations. See **A-Z**.

MICHAELSKIRCHE Neuhauser Strasse 52.
U-Bahn 4, 5; S-Bahn Karlsplatz.
The largest 16thC Renaissance church and most important Counter-Reformation church in Germany. Sung Mass Sun. am. See **WALK 1**, **A-Z**.

PETERSKIRCHE Rindermarkt 1.
U-Bahn 3, 6; S-Bahn Marienplatz.
Munich's oldest parish church was completely restored after the war. It houses a famous statue of St. Peter by Erasmus Grasser. See **WALK 2**, **A-Z**.

ASAMKIRCHE Sendlinger Strasse 62.
U-Bahn 1-3, 6 Sendlinger Tor.
Notable for its lavishly decorated rococo interior by the Asam brothers (see **A-Z***). You will either love it or hate it! See* **WALK 1**, **A-Z**.

LUDWIGSKIRCHE Ludwigstrasse 20.
U-Bahn 3, 6 Universität; bus 53.
University church, built between 1829 and 1844, which contains a huge fresco, The Last Judgement by Cornelius.

THEATINERKIRCHE Theatinerstrasse 22.
U-Bahn 3-6 Odeonsplatz. Beside the Feldherrnhalle.
Huge, copper-domed church in Italian high-baroque style with a rococo façade by Cuvilliés (see **A-Z***) and a plain white interior. See* **WALK 3**.

DREIFALTIGKEITSKIRCHE (TRINITY CHURCH)
Pacellistrasse 6. U-Bahn 4, 5; S-Bahn Karlsplatz.
The only church in the city to escape war damage, Dreifaltigkeitskirche ranks high architecturally among Bavaria's baroque churches. It features an elegant convex façade and a dome fresco, Holy Trinity (1715), by Cosmas Damian Asam (see **A-Z***). See* **WALK 3**.

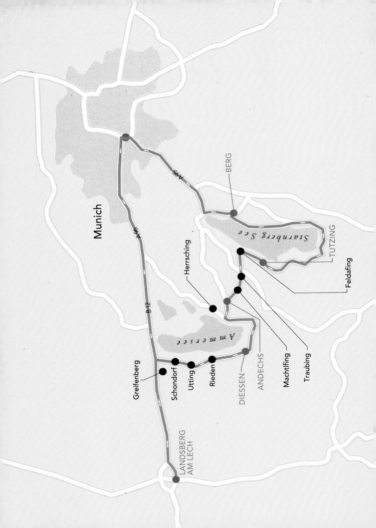

EXCURSION 1

A one-day excursion southwest of Munich taking in the town of Landsberg am Lech and the lakeside resorts of Ammersee and Starnberger See.

Join the A 96 autobahn (motorway) at the Mittlerer Ring by Westpark, which becomes the B 12 and then the B 96 (E 54).

55 km – Landsberg am Lech (see **A-Z**). An attractive fortress town lying between Swabia and Bavaria, which retains much of its medieval character.

Take the B 12 back towards Ammersee and turn right at Greifenberg to join the lakeside road running south through the villages of Schondorf, Utting and Rieden.

90 km – Diessen. A pleasant resort with a park on the southwest shore of the Ammersee, offering plenty of opportunities for water sports. Visit the church dominating the town, one of Johann Michael Fischer's most mature late-baroque works, containing a dramatic high altar by Cuvilliés (see **A-Z**), sculptures by Straub (see **A-Z**), a painting of the Crucifixion by Georges Desmarées and a wooden statue of St. Peter by Erasmus Grasser. Continue following the road round the lake towards Herrsching on the eastern side. Just before Herrsching take the road to the right leading up to Andechs.

105 km – Andechs (see **A-Z**). Famous for its Benedictine abbey. Its attractive courtyards and beer gardens make Andechs a popular weekend destination from Munich. Take the southeast road via Machtlfing and Traubing to Feldafing on Starnberger See. After crossing the railway line follow the southern road running parallel to the lake shore.

125 km – Tutzing. Pleasant resort on this 20-km-long lake whose shores are lined with the luxurious villas of many public figures. A boat service operates from here. Continue driving round the lake.

155 km – Berg. Schloss Berg on the eastern shore of the lake dates from 1640 and has the distinction of being the royal palace where Ludwig II spent his last days, in virtual captivity. A cross in the water, beside a chapel by the woods, marks the spot where he mysteriously drowned three days after being deposed.

Keep going on the same road and join the A 95 (E 533) autobahn (motorway) back to Munich.

Munich

Starnberg

Weilheim
Peissenberg

Peiting

STEINGADEN
ROTTENBUCH

WIESKIRCHE

SCHLOSS
LINDERHOF
ETTAL

Füssen
OBERAMMERGAU
Oberau

NEUSCHWANSTEIN

HOHENSCHWANGAU

Lech

Ammersee

Starnberger See

Lech

EXCURSION 2

A one- to two-day excursion to the abbeys, churches and castles (in particular the royal castles of Neuschwanstein and Hohenschwangau) of Bavaria as well as the famous town of Oberammergau.

Join the A 95 (E 533) Garmisch-Partenkirchen autobahn (motorway) at the Mittlerer Ring (Luise-Liesselbach-Platz). Turn off to the right at Oberau after 68 km and head north on the B 23 known as the Deutsche Alpenstrasse.

75 km – Ettal (see **A-Z**). A village made famous by its Benedictine abbey church (0800-1800). Continue along the same road on leaving the monastery and take the first turning on the left.

86 km – Schloss Linderhof (see **A-Z**). Ludwig II's favourite castle (0900-1215, 1245-1730 summer; 1000-1215, 1245-1600 winter; DM 6). Go back to Ettal and turn left at the T-junction to rejoin the B 23.

101 km – Oberammergau. This charming town, with its painted houses, is a famous woodcarving centre and its shop windows are full of the traditional religious figures in which it specializes. The town is, of course, also famous for the passion play held here every ten years (May-Sep.) to commemorate the community's miraculous preservation from the plague of 1634. The theatre can be visited when the play is not running 1000-1200, 1400-1600 Tue.-Sun. Continue north on the B 23, crossing the Echelsbach Bridge over a deep river gorge.

102 km – Rottenbuch. Famous for its church, the Maria-Geburt-Kirche (Church of the Nativity of the Virgin), which was originally built by Augustinian monks and rebuilt in the 15thC in late-Gothic style. In the 18thC it was remodelled in baroque and rococo styles and richly decorated with stuccowork by Josef Schmuzer and frescoes by Matthäus Günther. Return along the road you came on and turn right in the direction of Steingaden just after the bridge. Take the road branching off to the left after about 7.5 km.

132 km – Wieskirche (see **A-Z**). Considered to be a masterpiece of German rococo ecclesiastical architecture, this church stands alone in its meadows in attractive countryside (0800-1800). Return to the main

road and carry on in a westerly direction.

138 km – Steingaden. Visit the abbey church of St. Johann Baptist dating from the 12thC (0800-1800). Although later remodelled in baroque style, the exterior, with its solid tower and Lombard arcades, has retained its original Romanesque flavour. The frescoes illustrate the history of the Guelfs, the local rulers, one of whom founded the church before departing on crusade. Follow the B 17 from here towards Füssen, turning off to the left several kilometres before the town.

158 km – Neuschwanstein and Hohenschwangau. The former, visible from the road, is truly a fairy-tale castle, with its towers and pinnacles. Building began in 1869 and was inspired by the palace of Versailles and the castle of Wartburg, both favourites of Ludwig II. The decor is dominated by allusions to Wagnerian operatic themes. The castle's magnificent hilltop setting and mountain backdrop can best be appreciated from the Marienbrücke across the Pöllat gorge, which can be reached from a path behind the building. The yellow 12thC edifice on the hill opposite Ludwig II's dream castle is Hohenschwangau (0900-1730 summer, 1000-1600 winter; DM 7). His mother Queen Marie lived here for many years, and it was here that he grew up. Although built on a much more modest scale, this castle is perhaps more interesting for its domestic, everyday characteristics. The Wagnerian motifs are still present, but in a less prominent and more varied form. Some of the main features include Biedermeier furniture, murals based on Schwind cartoons of medieval heroic chronicles, and various works of art received by the royal family from different parts of Bavaria. The stars in the night sky painted on the ceiling of Ludwig II's bedroom were designed to light up.

Return to the B 17 and drive north to Peiting where you should keep straight on for the B 472 to pass through Peissenberg. Turn left just after the town and head for Weilheim to join the northbound B 2 to Starnberg. Here you can rejoin the A 952 and then the A 95 (E 533) Garmisch-Partenkirchen autobahn (motorway), taking you straight back to Munich.

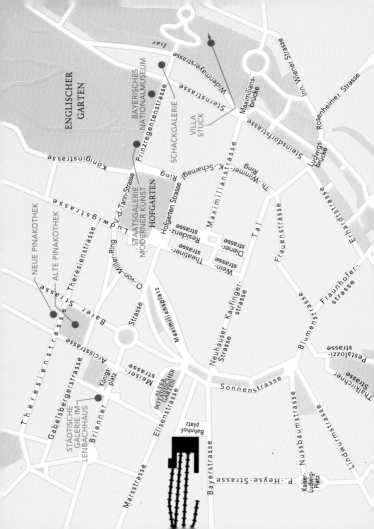

ENGLISCHER
GARTEN

Isar

Widenmayerstrasse

BAYERISCHES
NATIONALMUSEUM

Prinzregentenstrasse

Sternstrasse

Maximilians-
brücke

Steinsdorfstrasse

Ludwigs-
brücke

Rosenheimer Strasse

Am Wiener Platz

SCHACKGALERIE

VILLA
STUCK

Königinstrasse

Th.-Wimmer-Schwanthaler-Ring

Maximilianstrasse

STAATSGALERIE
MODERNER KUNST

V.-d.-Tann-Strasse

Ludwigstrasse

Hofgarten Strasse

HOFGARTEN

Residenz-
strasse

Tal

Frauenstrasse

Ehrhardtstrasse

NEUE PINAKOTHEK

ALTE PINAKOTHEK

Theresienstrasse

O.-von-Miller-Ring

Theater-
strasse

Diener-
strasse

Wein-
strasse

Kaufinger-
strasse

Neuhauser
Strasse

Fraunhofer-
strasse

Barer Strasse

Strasse

Arcisstrasse

Maximiliansplatz

Blumenstrasse

Pestalozzi-
strasse

Theresienstrasse

Meiser-
strasse

Königs-
platz

ALTER
BOTANISCHER
GARTEN

Elisenstrasse

Sonnenstrasse

Nussbaumstrasse

Lindwurmstrasse

Thalkirchner
Strasse

STÄDTISCHE
GALERIE IM
LENBACHHAUS

Gabelsbergerstrasse

Brienner

Bahnhof-
platz

Marsstrasse

Bayerstrasse

P.-Heyse-Strasse

Kaiser-
Ludwig-
Platz

BAYERISCHES NATIONALMUSEUM Prinzregentenstrasse 3.
❑ 0930-1700 Tue.-Sun. Bus 53, 55. ❑ DM 3, free Sun. & hol.
Tremendously varied and individual art collection, including one of the largest collections of German sculpture. See **A-Z**.

ALTE PINAKOTHEK Barer Strasse 27.
• ❑ 0900-1630 Tue.-Sun. (also 1900-2100 Tue., Thu.).
U-Bahn 2 Theresienstrasse; tram 18. ❑ DM 4, free Sun. & hol.
Munich's most famous gallery rivals the Louvre and the Prado. It contains the Royal Collection of European art up to the 18thC. See **A-Z**.

NEUE PINAKOTHEK Barer Strasse 29.
❑ 0900-1630 Tue.-Sun. (also 1900-2100 Tue., Thu.).
U-Bahn 2 Theresienstrasse; tram 18. ❑ DM 4, free Sun. & hol.
Houses an important collection of 19thC art. See **A-Z**.

STAATSGALERIE MODERNER KUNST Haus der Kunst,
Prinzregentenstrasse 1.
❑ 0900-1630 Tue.-Sun. (also 1900-2100 Thu.). Bus 53, 55.
In the west wing. ❑ DM 3.50, free Sun. & hol.
All the most important artists and schools of the 20thC are represented.

SCHACKGALERIE Prinzregentenstrasse 9.
❑ 0900-1630 Wed.-Mon. Bus 53, 55. ❑ DM 2.50, free Sun. & hol.
Features German 19thC romantic and post-romantic paintings. Artists include Böcklin, Feuerbach, Lenbach, Schwind and Spitzweg.

STÄDTISCHE GALERIE IM LENBACHHAUS Luisenstrasse 33.
❑ 1000-1800 Tue.-Sun. U-Bahn 2 Königsplatz. ❑ DM 4.
19th-20thC paintings include works of the Blauer Reiter group, German forerunners of abstractionism. See **BUILDINGS 2**, **WALK 3**, **Lenbachhaus**.

VILLA STUCK Prinzregentenstrasse 60.
❑ Special exhibitions only 1000-1700 (until 2230 Thu.). Tram 18, bus 53.
Painter Franz von Stuck's neoclassical villa, decorated by himself, houses an Art Nouveau museum full of interesting turn-of-the-century items.

RESIDENZMUSEUM Residenz, Max-Joseph-Platz 3.
❑ 1000-1630 Tue.-Sat., 1000-1300 Sun. Morning and afternoon guided tours. U-Bahn 3-6 Odeonsplatz; S-Bahn Marienplatz. ❑ DM 3.50.
Visit over 112 rooms in the fabulous royal residence. See **WALK 3**.

SCHATZKAMMER (TREASURY) Residenz, Max-Joseph-Platz 3.
❑ 1000-1300 Tue.-Sat., 1000-1300 Sun. U-Bahn 3-6 Odeonsplatz; S-Bahn Marienplatz. ❑ DM 3.50, free Sun. & hol.
The Wittelsbach treasures: crowns, jewels, ivory, and much more.

STAATLICHE ANTIKENSAMMLUNG Königsplatz 1.
❑ 1000-1630 Tue., Thu.-Sun., 1200-2030 Wed. U-Bahn 2 Königsplatz.
❑ DM 3.50, free Sun. & hol.
Impressive collection of Greek, Etruscan and Roman artefacts. See **A-Z**.

GLYPTOTHEK Königsplatz 3.
❑ 1000-1630 Tue., Wed., Fri.-Sun., 1200-2030 Thu. U-Bahn 2 Königspl.
❑ DM 6 (includes entrance to Antikensammlung), free Sun. & hol.
Fine neoclassical building housing one of the best collections of ancient sculpture in Europe. Important exhibits include the Barberini Faun.

MÜNCHNER STADTMUSEUM St.-Jakobs-Platz 1.
❑ 1000-1700 Tue., Thu.-Sun., 1000-2030 Wed. U-Bahn 1, 2, 3, 6 Marienplatz, Sendlinger Tor; S-Bahn Marienplatz. ❑ DM 4, free Sun. & hol.
Fascinating displays illustrating the history of Munich. See **WALK 2**, **A-Z**.

BAYERISCHE STAATSBIBLIOTHEK Ludwigstrasse 16.
❑ Temporary exhibitions 0900-1930 Mon.-Fri., 0900-1630 Sat.
U-Bahn 3, 6 Universität.
Over five million volumes, including 58,000 handwritten manuscripts and the biggest Oriental collection in Europe.

DEUTSCHES MUSEUM Museumsinsel 1.
❑ 0900-1700. S-Bahn Isartor; tram 18, 19. ❑ DM 5, Zeiss Planetarium an extra DM 1.50.
One of the world's largest science and technology museums. See **A-Z**.

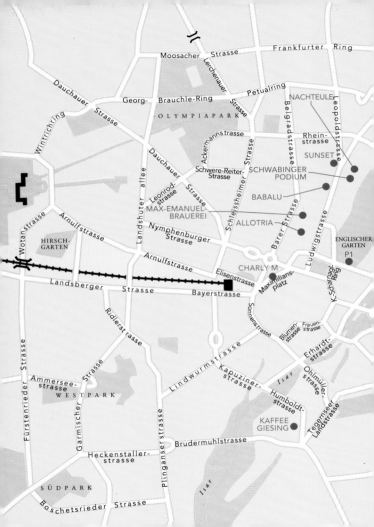

CHARLY M Regina-Haus, Maximiliansplatz 5.
❑ 2200-0400. U-Bahn 4, 5; S-Bahn Karlsplatz.
Quite an upmarket disco favoured by a young crowd.

P1 Prinzregentenstrasse 1.
❑ 2300-0400. Bus 5, 55.
Munich's top trendsetting disco. Only those with the 'right look' get in.

SUNSET Leopoldstrasse 69.
❑ 2000-0400. U-Bahn 3, 6 Münchener Freiheit.
Good mixture of music catering for most tastes.

NACHTEULE Occamstrasse 7.
❑ 1900-0100. U-Bahn 3, 6 Münchener Freiheit.
More of a cosy pub with dancing than a disco. Specializes in golden oldies but is popular with all age groups.

ALLOTRIA Türkenstrasse 33.
❑ 2000-0100 (from 1200 Sun.). U-Bahn 3, 6 Universität.
Mainstream jazz and Dixie plus rock 'n' roll night. Atmospheric, busy.

SCHWABINGER PODIUM Wagnerstrasse 1.
❑ 2000-0100 (from 1800 Sun.). U-Bahn 3, 6 Münchener Freiheit.
Mainly traditional jazz. Cosy spot with a good atmosphere.

BABALU Leopoldstrasse 19.
❑ 2100-0400. U-Bahn 3, 6 Giselastrasse.
Live music, largely performed by internationally known visiting bands.

MAX-EMANUEL-BRAUEREI Adalbertstrasse 33.
❑ 1100-0100. U-Bahn 3, 6 Universität.
Varied programme, including jazz, rock 'n' roll, salsa and Irish folk.

KAFFEE GIESING Bergstrasse 5/9.
❑ 1000-0100. U-Bahn 1, 2 Silberhornstrasse.
A mixture of everything you could imagine – folk, jazz, pop, etc.

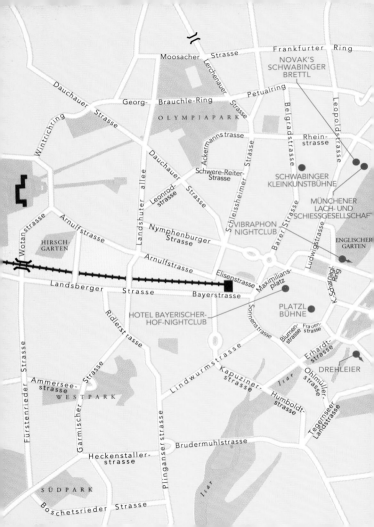

PLATZL BÜHNE Münzstrasse 8/9.
❏ Bookings: 1100-1800 Mon.-Sat., show starts 2000.
U-Bahn 3, 6; S-Bahn Marienplatz.
Bavarian music and humorous sketches go to make up a show which is a favourite with tourists.

MÜNCHENER LACH- UND SCHIESSGESELLSCHAFT
Haimhauserstrasse/Ursulastrasse corner.
❏ Bookings from 1400, show starts 2000.
U-Bahn 3, 6 Münchener Freiheit.
Top performers feature in the political cabaret in this small and very popular venue.

SCHWABINGER KLEINKUNSTBÜHNE Theater bei Heppel & Ettlich, Kaiserstrasse 67.
❏ Bookings from 1700; show starts around 2030.
U-Bahn 3, 6 Münchener Freiheit.
International guest stars appear in an enjoyably varied cabaret.

DREHLEIER Balanstrasse 23.
❏ Show starts around 2030 (booking essential).
S-Bahn Rosenheimer Platz.
Political cabaret with international guest stars. Popular and crowded, with a good atmosphere.

NOVAK'S SCHWABINGER BRETTL Occamstrasse 11.
❏ Show starts 2100. U-Bahn 3, 6 Münchener Freiheit.
Shows feature a wide range of international performers and good music.

VIBRAPHON NIGHTCLUB Sheraton Hotel, Arabellastrasse 6.
❏ 2200-0400 Tue.-Sat. U-Bahn 4 Richard-Strauss-Strasse.
Nightclub and upmarket disco with a more mature clientele.

HOTEL BAYERISCHER-HOF-NIGHTCLUB Promenadeplatz 2/6.
❏ 2030-0300. Tram 19, 29.
Sophisticated nightclub with good live dance music.

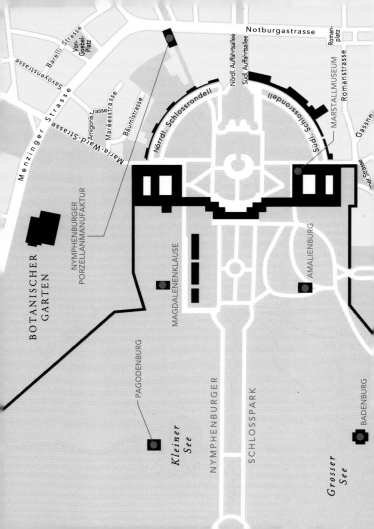

Notburgastrasse

Barelli Strasse

Von-Goebel-Platz

Savoyenstrasse

Romanplatz

Menzinger Strasse

Maria-Ward-Strasse

Amigonistrasse

Maréesstrasse

Bäumlstrasse

Romanstrasse

Gassne

Nördl. Auffahrtsallee

Südl. Auffahrtsallee

MARSTALLMUSEUM

Nördl. Schlossrondell

Südl. Schlossrondell

er Strasse

BOTANISCHER GARTEN

NYMPHENBURGER PORZELLANMANUFAKTUR

MAGDALENENKLAUSE

AMALIENBURG

PAGODENBURG

NYMPHENBURGER

SCHLOSSPARK

BADENBURG

Kleiner See

Grosser See

AMALIENBURG
❏ 0900-1230, 1330-1700 summer, 1000-1230, 1330-1600 winter.
❏ DM 2.
*A hunting lodge by Cuvilliés (see **A-Z**) and one of the most beautiful little rococo palaces in Germany. Magnificent circular Hall of Mirrors.*

BADENBURG
❏ 1000-1230, 1330-1700 Tue.-Sat. (summer). ❏ DM 2.
*Bathing pavilion by Effner (see **A-Z**) with a large, heated swimming pool lined with Delft tiles. Adjacent rooms in once-fashionable Chinese style.*

PAGODENBURG
❏ 1000-1230, 1330-1700 Tue.-Sun. ❏ DM 1.
*An attractive two-storeyed octagonal building also by Effner (see **A-Z**). The ground-floor room is decorated with Dutch tiles and ceiling paintings by G. Gumpp. See the delightful Chinese Cabinet upstairs.*

MAGDALENENKLAUSE
❏ 1000-1230, 1330-1700 Tue.-Sun. ❏ DM 1.
*Designed by Effner (see **A-Z**) for Elector Max Emanuel, to resemble a ruin. The chapel, decorated with shells and coral, resembles a grotto.*

MARSTALLMUSEUM
❏ 0900-1230, 1330-1700 Tue.-Sun. (summer), 1000-1230, 1330-1600 Tue.-Sun. (winter). South wing of main palace. ❏ DM 2.
Magnificent ceremonial coaches and sleighs belonging to Bavarian royalty. Don't miss the coronation coach of Elector Karl Albrecht.

NYMPHENBURGER PORZELLANMANUFAKTUR
❏ 0800-1200, 1230-1700 Mon.-Fri. Closed hol. Roundel on north side.
The famous porcelain factory has a showroom where china is sold.

NYMPHENBURGER SCHLOSSPARK
❏ 0600-dusk. ❏ Free.
Originally landscaped in the Italianate manner, then in an ornamental French style, the park became anglicized and less formal in the 19thC.

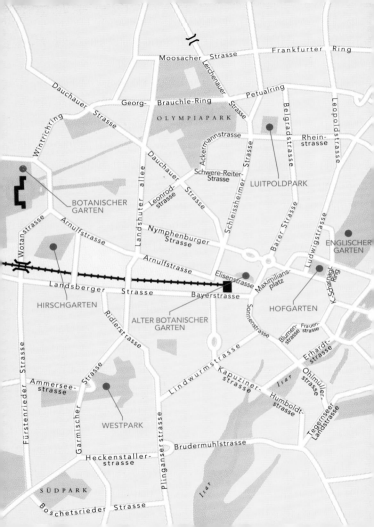

PARKS & GARDENS

ENGLISCHER GARTEN
❏ Always open. U-Bahn 3-6 Odeonsplatz; tram 20; bus 53. ❏ Free.
Wonderful park in the city centre with something for everyone. See **A-Z**.

BOTANISCHER GARTEN Menzinger Strasse 63.
❏ 0900-1800, hothouses 0900-1145, 1300-1730 (1 hr earlier in winter). Tram 12. ❏ DM 2.
A 1914 creation by Holfelder which successfully blends scientific and aesthetic interests. The hothouse contains beautiful water lilies. See **A-Z**.

ALTER BOTANISCHER GARTEN Between Elisenstrasse and
Sophienstrasse. ❏ Always open. U-Bahn 4, 5; S-Bahn Karlspl. ❏ Free.
Dominated by a massive fountain by Wackerle. A pleasant place to linger after errands in the city. See **A-Z**.

HOFGARTEN Between Odeonsplatz and Prinzregentenstrasse.
❏ Always open. U-Bahn 3-6 Odeonsplatz. ❏ Free.
Formal, French-style Renaissance garden with a series of radiating paths, fountains and seats. See **A-Z**.

WESTPARK Just off the westbound autobahn (motorway).
❏ Always open. U-Bahn 6 Westpark. ❏ Free.
An oasis of green created for the International Horticultural Festival (1983) and landscaped with hills. Features a rose garden, lake with open-air theatre, concert arena and playgrounds.

HIRSCHGARTEN Between Arnulfstrasse and the railway lines.
❏ Always open. S-Bahn Laim; bus 32, 41, 68. ❏ Free.
This park is particularly well known for its large, rambling beer garden, situated next to the deer enclosure which gave it its name. See **A-Z**.

LUITPOLDPARK Karl-Theodor-Strasse.
❏ Always open. U-Bahn 2, 3 Scheidplatz; tram 18. ❏ Free.
Given as a gift to the regent Prince Luitpold on his 90th birthday in 1911, this attractive park offers an unusual vantage point from the Schwabinger Schüttberg hill which was built of wartime rubble. See **A-Z**.

ENGLISCHER
GARTEN

PREYSING
KELLER

Inn.Wiener Strasse

Rosenheimer Strasse

Widenmayerstrasse

Isar

Sternstrasse

KÄFER-
SCHÄNKE

Prinzregentenstrasse

Maximilians-
brücke

Ludwigs-
brücke

Steinsdorfstrasse

HUNSLINGER

Königinstrasse

Th.-Wimmer-Ring

Schrag.-Ring

Maximilianstrasse

WALTERSPIEL

Erhardtstrasse

HOFGARTEN

Ludwigstrasse

V.-d.-Tann-Strasse

Hofgartenstrasse

Residenz-
strasse

Wein-
strasse

Diener-
strasse

Tal

Frauenstrasse

GRÜNE GANS

TANTRIS

Theresienstrasse

O.-von-Miller-Ring

Theater-
strasse

BOETTNER

Kaufinger-
strasse

Blumenstrasse

Fraunhofer-
strasse

Pestalozzi-
strasse

Bayer Strasse

Theresienstrasse

Arcisstrasse

Strasse

Maximiliansplatz

Neuhauser
Strasse

Sonnenstrasse

Thalkirchner
Strasse

Gabelsbergerstrasse

Königs-
platz

Meiser
strasse

ALTER
BOTANISCHER
GARTEN

Elisenstrasse

Nussbaumstrasse

Lindwurmstrasse

Brienner

Marsstrasse

AUBERGINE

Bahnhof-
platz

Kaiser-
Ludwig-
Platz

P.-Heyse-Strasse

Bayerstrasse

AUBERGINE Maximiliansplatz 5.
❑ 1200-1400, 1900-0100 Tue.-Sat. Closed two weeks in Aug.
U-Bahn 4, 5; S-Bahn Karlsplatz. ❑ Expensive.
Innovative German cuisine and fine wines in Munich's best restaurant.

BOETTNER Theatinerstrasse 8.
❑ 1100-2400 Mon.-Sat. (till 0100 Sat.). Closed hol.
U-Bahn 3, 6; S-Bahn Marienplatz. ❑ Expensive.
Established, traditional Munich restaurant with an elegant atmosphere.

KÄFER-SCHÄNKE Prinzregentenstrasse 73.
❑ 1130-2315 Mon.-Sat. Closed hol. Tram 18; bus 55. ❑ Expensive.
An attractive setting, a daily-changing menu and a good range of wines.

WALTERSPIEL Hotel Vier Jahreszeiten, Maximilianstrasse 17.
❑ 1800-2400 Mon.-Fri. U-Bahn 3, 6; S-Bahn Marienplatz; tram 19, 29.
❑ Expensive.
Elegant, international gourmet restaurant in Munich's top hotel.

TANTRIS Johann-Fichte-Strasse 7.
❑ 1200-1400, 1830-2230 Tue.-Fri., 1830-2230 Sat., Mon.
U-Bahn 6 Dietlindenstrasse. ❑ Expensive.
Quality service, trendy decor, French nouvelle and international cuisine.

GRÜNE GANS Am Einlass 5.
❑ 1930-0100 Sun.-Fri. Closed three weeks Aug.
U-Bahn 3, 6; S-Bahn Marienplatz. ❑ Expensive.
*Small and cosy. Traditional Bavarian dishes (see **Food**) with French wine.*

PREYSING KELLER Innere Wiener Strasse 6.
❑ 1800-0100 Mon.-Sat. S-Bahn Rosenheimer Pl.; tram 18. ❑ Expensive.
Rustic, cellar restaurant serving classic French cuisine and good wines.

HUNSLINGER Braunstrasse 6.
❑ 1200-1500, 1830-0100 Mon.-Sat. Tram 15, 25. ❑ Expensive.
French cuisine with the emphasis on fish dishes.

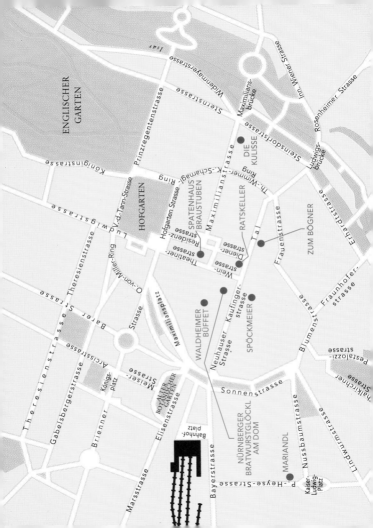

RATSKELLER Rathaus, Marienplatz 8.
❏ 0900-2400. U-Bahn 3, 6; S-Bahn Marienplatz. ❏ Moderate.
Enormous restaurant in the Rathaus cellar. Good for lunch, a special meal or just a pleasant glass of wine. A menu in English is available.

SPÖCKMEIER Rosenstrasse 9.
❏ 0900-2400. U-Bahn 3, 6; S-Bahn Marienplatz. ❏ Moderate.
Large restaurant on two floors serving a wide range of Bavarian (see **Food***) and international dishes.*

ZUM BÖGNER Tal 72.
❏ 0900-2400. U-Bahn 3, 6; S-Bahn Marienplatz. ❏ Moderate.
Bavarian restaurant (see **Food***) in the Munich tradition: large, popular and welcoming, especially to groups.*

NÜRNBERGER BRATWURSTGLÖCKL AM DOM
Frauenplatz 9. U-Bahn 3, 6; S-Bahn Marienplatz. ❏ Moderate.
Popular, cosy Bavarian restaurant (see **Food***) with bags of atmosphere.*

SPATENHAUS BRAUSTUBEN Residenzstrasse 12.
❏ 1000-0030. U-Bahn 3, 6; S-Bahn Marienplatz. ❏ Moderate.
More expensive, but serving a good range of international and Bavarian dishes (see **Food***).*

DIE KULISSE Maximilianstrasse 26.
❏ 0930-0100 (from 1200 Sun.). U-Bahn 3, 6; S-Bahn Marienplatz; tram 19, 29. Next to the Kammerspiele theatre. ❏ Moderate.
An international-style restaurant, café and bar with a warm atmosphere.

WALDHEIMER BÜFFET Löwengrube 18.
❏ 1000-2200. U-Bahn 3, 6; S-Bahn Marienpl.; tram 19, 29. ❏ Moderate.
International cuisine, pleasant atmosphere, courtyard and piano music.

MARIANDL Goethestrasse 51.
❏ 1100-0030 Mon.-Fri. U-Bahn 3, 6 Goetheplatz. ❏ Moderate.
Turn-of-the-century atmosphere and live classical music.

KYTARO Innere Wiener Strasse 36.
❑ 1700-0100. Tram 18. ❑ Inexpensive.
Busy Greek restaurant – live music, large tables and a good atmosphere.

BARDOLINO Fraunhoferstrasse 2.
❑ 1130-1430, 1730-2300 Sun.-Fri. U-Bahn 1, 2 Fraunhoferstrasse; tram 18, 20. Entrance in Müllerstrasse. ❑ Inexpensive.
A friendly restaurant mainly serving Italian dishes. Children welcome.

ITALY Leopoldstrasse 108.
❑ 1130-2400. U-Bahn 3, 6 Münchener Freiheit. ❑ Inexpensive.
Book ahead for this popular Italian restaurant with its pretty courtyard.

OPATIJA Brienner Strasse 41.
❑ 1100-2400. U-Bahn 2 Königsplatz. ❑ Inexpensive.
Oldest Yugoslavian restaurant in Munich. Good food in pleasant setting.

MAHARANI Rottmannstrasse 24.
❑ 1200-1500, 1800-2400. U-Bahn 1 Stiglmaierplatz. ❑ Inexpensive.
Good Indian food at reasonable prices. Excellent vegetarian dishes.

ZUNG-HUA Bayerstrasse 33.
❑ 1100-2300. U-Bahn 1, 2, 4, 5; S-Bahn Hauptbahnhof. ❑ Inexpensive.
Friendly Chinese restaurant offering attentive service and good prices.

ROSENWIRTH Brienner Strasse 50.
❑ 1100-2400. U-Bahn 1 Stiglmaierplatz. ❑ Inexpensive.
Large, reasonably priced Swiss restaurant. Pleasant terrace in summer.

PALENQUE Widenmayerstrasse 52.
❑ 1800-0100. Tram 20; bus 54. ❑ Inexpensive.
Attractive Mexican restaurant. Occasional live music.

AMARANTH Steinstrasse 42.
❑ 1800-2400. S-Bahn Rosenheimer Platz. ❑ Inexpensive.
Good, small vegetarian restaurant in simple surroundings. Very popular.

KAUFHOF Marienplatz.
U-Bahn 3, 6; S-Bahn Marienplatz.
*Large department store with a wide range of merchandise in its gift
department. See* **WALK 1**.

MÜNCHNER GESCHENKE-STUBEN Marienplatz 8.
U-Bahn 3, 6; S-Bahn Marienplatz. Entrance in Dienerstrasse.
*Sells a great range of souvenirs – anything from traditional nutcrackers to
bunches of Bavarian dried flowers.*

WALLACH HAUS FÜR VOLKSKUNST UND TRACHT
Residenzstrasse 3. U-Bahn 3, 6; S-Bahn Marienplatz.
Elegant store specializing in traditional Bavarian dress (see **Best Buys***).*

SEBASTIAN WESELY WACHSWAREN Rindermarkt 1.
U-Bahn 3, 6; S-Bahn Marienplatz. Behind Peterskirche.
*Oldest establishment in Munich, selling candles, figures and wax
pictures.*

KARL STORR OBERAMMERGAU HOLZSCHNITZKUNST
Kaufingerstrasse 25. U-Bahn 3, 6; S-Bahn Marienplatz.
*Carries a fine selection of good-quality Oberammergau woodcarvings
(see* **EXCURSION 2***).*

LEUTE Viktualienmarkt 15.
U-Bahn 3, 6; S-Bahn Marienplatz. Corner of Viktualienmarkt.
Sells a wide range of wooden articles and gifts.

HAERTLE Neuhauser Strasse 9.
U-Bahn 3, 6; S-Bahn Marienplatz. Entrance in passage.
Offers an excellent range of porcelain and glassware.

HUT BREITER Kaufingerstrasse.
U-Bahn 3, 6; S-Bahn Marienplatz.
*One branch of a chain of shops which specialize in selling traditional
Bavarian hats.*

MEDIA MARKT Ingolstädter Strasse 62.
Bus 85.
Quality TVs, hi-fis and electrical goods at very reasonable prices. See
Best Buys.

HUGENDUBEL Marienplatz 22.
U-Bahn 3, 6; S-Bahn Marienplatz.
*Attractive bookshop with a good selection of English-language books.
See* **WALK 2**.

SCHLICHTING Weinstrasse 8.
U-Bahn 3, 6; S-Bahn Marienplatz.
Upmarket store carrying everything for children, including clothes.

OBLETTER Marienplatz 19.
U-Bahn 3, 6; S-Bahn Marienplatz.
Large, two-storey toy shop with a range of fun and educational toys.

LODEN-FREY Maffeistrasse 79.
U-Bahn 3, 6; S-Bahn Marienplatz.
The traditional textile king of Munich. Bavarian dress a speciality (see
Best Buys*).*

BECK Marienplatz 11.
U-Bahn 3, 6; S-Bahn Marienplatz.
Clothing, cosmetics and fabrics sold in one of Munich's best stores.

WOM Kaufingerstrasse 15.
U-Bahn 4, 5; S-Bahn Karlsplatz.
Particularly good for modern music of all categories.

SPORT-SCHECK Sendlinger Strasse 85.
U-Bahn 3, 6; S-Bahn Marienplatz.
*Sports shop on five floors and featuring a 22-m-high training wall for
climbers. The assistants can arrange courses, lessons, bookings, etc. for
you (see* **Sports***).*

SHOPPING 3

DALLMAYR Dienerstrasse 22.
U-Bahn 3, 6; S-Bahn Marienplatz.
One of the leading European grocery establishments and worth a visit just to walk around the hall with its marble columns and fountain. Everything from caviar to Bavarian specialities is sold here. Especially well known for its delicious coffee.

HERTIE Bahnhofplatz 7.
U-Bahn 1, 2, 4, 5; S-Bahn Hauptbahnhof.
A huge department store with a good delicatessen in the basement where, if you are feeling homesick, you can buy British Isles produce.

FEINKOST KÄFER Prinzregentenstrasse 73.
Tram 18; bus 55.
An extremely classy delicatessen with its own attractive restaurant, Käfer-Schänke (see **RESTAURANTS 1***).*

WERTKAUF Ingolstädter Strasse 58b.
Bus 85.
A discount hypermarket offering an excellent selection of wines.

NORDEND-QUELLE Nordendstrasse 52.
Tram 18.
Another store offering a good range of wines.

VIKTUALIENMARKT
Bus 52.
Fascinating food market selling every kind of fruit and vegetable imaginable, as well as wine, cheese, meat, fish, plants and flowers. It stands on the historic location of the city's first Benedictine settlement and the original site of the Peterskirche (see **CHURCHES**, **A-Z***). See* **WALK 2**, **Shopping***.*

ELISABETHMARKT Elisabethplatz 18.
Tram 18.
An atmospheric little food market in a pleasant setting on the edge of a small park in the trendy district of Schwabing (see **A-Z***).*

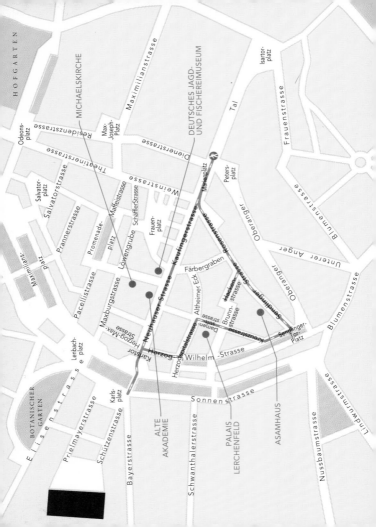

Neues Rathaus

Altes Rathaus

Begin your walk at Marienplatz (see **A-Z**) where you will see the impressive facades of the Altes and the Neues Rathaus (see **BUILDINGS 2, A-Z**). Try and time it to coincide with the performance of the famous Glockenspiel (see **A-Z**). Leaving the square with the Kaufhof department store (see **SHOPPING 1**) on your left, you enter Kaufingerstrasse. This main shopping area is a lively pedestrian precinct with plenty of street entertainment. It leads into Neuhauser Strasse where the statue of a wild boar stands at the entrance to the Deutsches Jagd- und Fischereimuseum (see **A-Z**) in the former Augustinerkirche at No. 53. Across the road is the Michaelskirche (see **CHURCHES**, **A-Z**). The adjacent building is a former Jesuit college, the Alte Akademie, dating back to 1585-87 and which is now owned by the University. On the corner stands the modern Richard Strauss Fountain decorated with scenes from his opera *Salome*. Opposite, at No. 16, is the Augustinerbräu (see **BEER CELLARS**), a brewery founded in 1328. The Bürgersaal, the 18thC place of worship of the Marian Congregation, is at No. 48 (1100-1300), with the restored meeting hall upstairs and the small chapel downstairs. On your right, before you reach the Karlstor (see **City Fortifications**), you will see the old department store of Oberpollinger which occupies a turn-of-the-century building by Max Littmann and has three gables decorated with craft symbols. It was here that the city's first beer-maker did his brewing. As you cross Herzog-Max-Strasse look out for the charming Brunnen-buberl, an Art-Nouveau fountain (1895) depicting a satyr spitting water over a small boy.

Carry straight on through the former city gate of Karlstor to the fountain on Karlsplatz (see **A–Z**) before retracing your steps back through the Karlstor and taking the first street on your right, Herzog-Wilhelm-Strasse. Next, turn first left onto Herzogspitalstrasse and note the original Empire facade with its attractive female heads at No. 12, all that remains of the Gregorian Seminar founded here in 1573 by Albrecht V. The Herzogspital church of St. Elisabeth at No. 9 is a modern church (although the tower dates from 1727-28) housing a wooden statue of Mary dating from 1651. The early-19thC building at No. 8 is the oldest wine tavern in Munich, the Weinhaus Neuner (now a quality restaurant). Turn right down Damenstiftstrasse. At No. 1 visit the Damenstift church of St. Anna with its 18thC Last Supper, a group of life-size figures next to the altar. At No. 8 is the ornate green-and-gold facade of the Palais Lerchenfeld, which dates from 1726 and today houses an undertakers. Carry on into the adjoining Kreuzstrasse, noticing as you do so the delightful stone sculpture, locally known as the *Madonna in a Pear Tree*, on the corner of Brunnstrasse. No. 10 Kreuzstrasse is the original address of the cemetery chapel of St. Peter's parish (now relocated) which was built in the 1400s by Jörg von Halsbach, the cathedral architect.

Continue along to the Sendlinger Tor (see **City Fortifications**), one of the three remaining city gates, which is now a busy traffic junction and the location of Munich's oldest cinema (1913), the Sendlinger-Tor-Filmtheater. Walk down Sendlinger Strasse towards Marienplatz and

admire the famous Asamhaus at No. 61 (see **BUILDINGS 2**, **A-Z**) and the Asamkirche at No. 62 (see **CHURCHES**, **A-Z**). Turn left at the priest's house at No. 63 into the Asamhof, a delightful modern courtyard with shops, cafés, original sculptures and fountains.

Return to Sendlinger Strasse and carry on to the corner of Hackenstrasse where you will find the Altes Hackerhaus at No. 75, a four-storeyed 19thC building with a charming courtyard and a classical columned facade which houses a restaurant and used to be the site of the old Hacker family brewery. On the opposite corner look for the copy of one of Grasser's famous Moorish dancers. The bells surrounding the statue chime every quarter of an hour.

Turn left into Hackenstrasse and you will see the imposing neoclassical

facade of the Radspielerhaus at No. 7. This former 17thC palace once belonged to the famous 19thC gilder, Joseph Radspieler, and has the only remaining garden courtyard in Munich. The Gaststätte zur Hundskugel a little further on is the oldest restaurant in Munich and dates back to 1440. The house at No. 10, one of the few remaining burgher houses of the late baroque period, was once owned by the sculptor Johann Baptist Straub (see **A-Z**). Return to Marienplatz by retracing your steps along Hackenstrasse, turning right into Sendlinger Strasse and continuing to the end of the road.

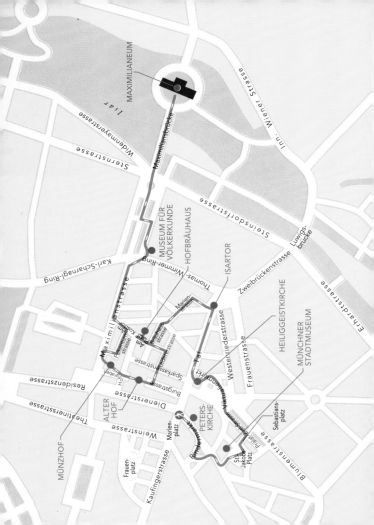

MAXIMILIANEUM

Isar

Widenmayerstrasse

Sternstrasse

Maximiliansbrücke

Inn. Wiener Strasse

Steinsdorfstrasse

Ludwigs-brücke

MUSEUM FÜR
VÖLKERKUNDE

HOFBRÄUHAUS

Karl-Scharnagl-Ring

Thomas-Wimmer-Ring

ISARTOR

Zweibrückenstrasse

Erhardtstrasse

Maximilianstrasse

Alfons-
strasse

Maffei-
strasse

Marienstrasse

Westenriederstrasse

HEILIGGEISTKIRCHE

MÜNCHNER
STADTMUSEUM

Residenzstrasse

Hochbrücken-
strasse

Sparkassenstrasse

Tal

Frauenstrasse

Theatinerstrasse

Sparkassenstrasse

Viktualienmarkt

Hofgraben

Burgstrasse

Dienerstrasse

ALTER
HOF

MÜNZHOF

Weinstrasse

Marien-
platz

PETERS-
KIRCHE

Rindermarkt

Sebastians-
platz

St. Jakobs-
Platz

Petersplatz

Blumenstrasse

Frauen-
platz

Kaufingerstrasse

WALK 2

Begin your walk at Marienplatz and take Rindermarkt to the left of Hugendubel (see **SHOPPING 2**) to visit the Peterskirche (see **CHURCHES, A-Z**). Climb the church tower, Alte Peter (see **A-Z**), for a good view of the city before continuing down the Rindermarkt and crossing over by the Maredo steakhouse to take a look at the Ruffinihäuser at No. 10. This block of three houses by Gabriel von Seidl dates from 1903-05 and is charmingly embellished with reliefs on blue and orange backgrounds. In front of it is the Rinderbrunnen (Cattle Fountain), decorated with figures of cattle – a popular place to linger. Walk round the bottom of this green area and cross Rindermarkt again at the Löwenturm (Lion Tower), a former water tower probably dating from the 16thC. Follow Rindermarkt down to St.-Jakobs-Platz. This spacious square was once the site of seasonal markets and is now the location of the Münchner Stadtmuseum (see **MUSEUMS 2, A-Z**) and the former residence (No. 15) of the influential rococo sculptor Ignaz Günther (1725-75). The latter is a fine example of a late-medieval burgher house. On the Oberanger side of the house is a copy of Günther's *House Madonna*, the original of which is in the Bayerisches Nationalmuseum (see **MUSEUMS 1, A-Z**). Go round the Stadtmuseum into Sebastiansplatz and take a look at the houses at No. 8 and 9 which have the half-gables once typical of Munich residences. The one at No. 8 also has a typical 'stairway to Heaven' – a straight staircase rising from ground level to the attic. Turn left into Prälat-Zistl-Strasse and cross over into Viktualienmarkt (see **SHOPPING 3**) which dates back to 1807 and has cafés, snack bars and a beer garden in summer around the maypole in addition to its numerous stalls. Of its several noteworthy fountains, look out in particular for the Fischbuberl-Brunnen on the west side, featuring the figure of a small boy clutching two fish. The market is particularly lively on the last day of Fasching (see **Events**).

Walk through the market in a northerly direction towards the Heiliggeistkirche (see **A-Z**). The row of butchers' shops on the opposite side of the road was built into the terrace below the Peterskirche (see **CHURCHES, A-Z**) in 1881 by Zenetti. Enter the Heiliggeistkirche by the side door and take a look around before turning right down Tal, a wide street lined with restaurants and furniture shops, which begins on the other side of the church. Walk straight down to the end of the street to

Heiliggeistkirche

one of the city's three remaining gates, the Isartor (see **City Fortifications**), which houses the Valentin-Musäum (see **A-Z**) in its southern tower. Then turn back towards Tal and take the first street on the right, Lueg ins Land, at the end of which stands the Vindeliker-Haus, incorporating a 14thC watchtower. Go left from here and walk up Marienstrasse. Cross over into Bräuhausstrasse and turn right into Am Platzl, a pedestrian precinct in front of which is situated one of Munich's most famous buildings, the Hofbräuhaus (see **BEER CELLARS**). Take the southerly Orlandostrasse (also a pedestrian precinct) out of Am Platzl and turn right into Ledererstrasse. Cross over Sparkassenstrasse, noticing the bridge across this street which, from 1800, connected the Altes Rathaus (see **BUILDINGS 2**, **A-Z**) with the Alter Hof (see **BUILDINGS 1**, **A-Z**). It was popularly known as the Bridge of Sighs because offenders had to cross it on the way to court or prison. The Zerwirkgewölbe at No. 3, dating from 1264, is the oldest venison and game shop in Bavaria.

Pass under the Schlichtinger arch into Burgstrasse. Opposite, at No. 5, is the Weinstadl (see **WINE TAVERNS**), a late-Gothic burgher house with facade paintings dating from 1552 and vaulted ceilings. The composer Mozart wrote *Idomeneo* at No. 7 and the architect Cuvilliés (see **A-Z**) lived at No. 8. Go north along Burgstrasse into the Alter Hof, coming out into Hofgraben to visit the Münzhof (0800-1615 Mon.-Fri.), site of the Hauptmünzamt (see **BUILDINGS 2**, **A-Z**). Turn left into Maximilianstrasse, a wide street laid out by King Maximilian I which is now lined with 'English Gothic'-style buildings housing elegant designer shops, galleries and antique shops. Turn right into Falkenturmstrasse, then left into Am Kosttor to see the Wolfsbrunnen (Wolf Fountain) on which the figures of Little Red Riding Hood and the infamous wolf stand. Return to Maximilianstrasse and turn right to walk past the 19thC Hotel Vier Jahreszeiten, Munich's most elegant address. Continue across the ring road to the Staatliches Museum für Völkerkunde (see **A-Z**), a massive Gothic-style building with an imposing facade. Lastly, cross over the Maximilian Bridge to the Maximilianeum (see **BUILDINGS 2**, **A-Z**), seat of the Bavarian Landtag. From here you can take U-Bahn 4 or 5 at Max-Weber-Platz and change at Odeonsplatz for line 3 or 6 to return to Marienplatz.

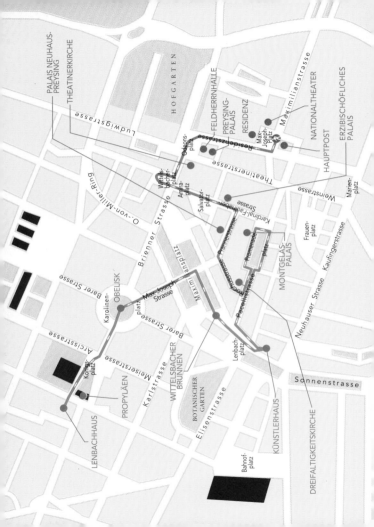

Begin your walk at Max-Joseph-Platz (see **A-Z**), the impressive location of the Hauptpost in the Palais Törring-Jettenbach (see **BUILDINGS 1**, **A-Z**), the Residenz (see **BUILDINGS 1**, **MUSEUMS 2**, **A-Z**) and the Nationaltheater (see **A-Z**). Walk north along Residenzstrasse past the Preysing-Palais (see **BUILDINGS 1**) which stands on the left at No. 27 just before the Odeonsplatz (see **A-Z**). The Feldherrnhalle (see **BUILDINGS 2**, **A-Z**) is on your left just as you enter the square. On the west side is the Theatinerkirche (see **CHURCHES**). Turn left into Brienner Strasse and you will come to Wittelsbacherplatz on your right, a spacious square flanked by elegant palaces. The centre of the square is dominated by the 19thC statue of Elector Maximilian I, constituting one of Munich's finest neoclassical monuments.

Turn left from here into Amiraplatz and, on the left-hand side, you will see the windows of the Vereinigte Werkstätten displaying the latest ideas in interior design. Carry on into Salvatorplatz, occupied by what was originally a cemetery church founded by Duke Albrecht V in 1493. The graves that were removed from here in 1789 are listed on a bronze plaque on the north wall where you can read the name of architect

Max-Joseph-Platz

François de Cuvilliés (see **A-Z**). Continue into Kardinal-Faulhaber-Strasse and look out for the Erzbischöfliches Palais (see **BUILDINGS 1**) at No. 7, and the Palais Portia (see **BUILDINGS 1**) at No. 12, among the elegant facades. Turn right into Prannerstrasse where you will see the 18thC Palais Neuhaus-Preysing at No. 2, the second town house of the Preysing counts. Continue past the other striking 18thC facades lining the street and turn left into Rochusstrasse. Walk beside the walls of the former Carmelite nunnery (you can visit the main courtyard in the Pacelli-Passage) and turn left into Pacellistrasse. Keep going past the Dreifaltigkeitskirche (see **CHURCHES**), on your left, into the Promenadeplatz where old and new buildings are juxtaposed around the long, oval, central area of green, the former site of a salt market. The four statues are of the composers Gluck and Orlando, the historian Westenrieder and Elector Max Emanuel II. The Montgelas-Palais (see

A-Z) is at the far end of the square on the left. Return to Pacellistrasse and take a look at the Maxburg Turm, a high tower which is all that remains of the Herzog-Max-Burg, a castle built between 1593 and 1596 for Wilhelm V. Turn left at Lenbachplatz and continue on to the Künstlerhaus at No. 8, once the social centre of Munich's artistic life, designed in the late 19thC by Gabriel von Siedl. Cross the square by the U-Bahn subway and then cross the road to admire the city's most beautiful fountain, the Wittelsbacher Brunnen (see **A-Z**). Walk through the park area behind the fountain and turn left at the next set of lights into Max-Joseph-Strasse, and then head straight into Karolinenplatz. The obelisk by Leo von Klenze in the centre of the square is a monument to the 30,000 Bavarian soldiers who died in the Russian campaign of 1812. The former Palais Törring-Seefeld at No. 4 was erected in 1812 for Crown Prince Ludwig and today serves as the administrative building of the state lottery.

Leave the square by Brienner Strasse, going west in the direction of Königsplatz (see **A-Z**). The street on the right, Arcisstrasse, is the location of what was Hitler's congress building (at No. 12), which is now a music college. This is where the famous Munich Pact between Germany, Britain, France and Italy was signed in 1938 to hand the Czechoslovakian Sudetenland over to Germany. Meiserstrasse on the left was the site of the former Nazi Party HQ (at No. 10) which now houses the Staatliche Graphische Sammlung, the State Graphic Collection (see **A-Z**). Head into Königsplatz (see **A-Z**) and cross over to the right of the Propyläen (see **BUILDINGS 2**) to look at the Lenbachhaus (see **BUILDINGS 2**, **MUSEUMS 1**, **A-Z**). To return to Marienplatz from here, catch U-Bahn 2 at Königsplatz and change at Sendlinger Tor.

ALTDEUTSCHE WEINSTUBE Tattenbachstrasse 6.
❑ 1900-0100 Tue.-Sun. U-Bahn 4, 5 Lehel.
Photos of actors and singers on the walls, live piano music and active participation by regular patrons who get up and sing.

PFÄLZER WEINPROBIERSTUBEN Residenz, Residenzstrasse 1.
❑ 1000-2400. U-Bahn 3-6 Odeonsplatz.
Wines from the Rhineland are served in an enormous tavern with a vaulted roof. Always crowded and full of atmosphere.

WEINSTADL Burgstrasse 5.
❑ 1000-2400 Mon.-Sat., 1600-2400 Sun. & hol.
U-Bahn 3, 6; S-Bahn Marienplatz.
This wine tavern on three floors features cosy cellar rooms and a pleasant, leafy courtyard. See **WALK 2***.*

WEINKELLER ST. MICHAEL Neuhauser Strasse 11.
❑ 1630-2400 Mon.-Sat. U-Bahn 3, 6; S-Bahn Marienplatz.
Buffet and Schrammelmusik (Viennese folk music).

PFÄLZER WEINKELLER AM DOM Frauenplatz 11.
❑ 1130-0030. U-Bahn 3, 6; S-Bahn Marienplatz.
A large cellar comprising several rooms. Includes a restaurant.

ZUM WEINTRÖDLER Brienner Strasse 10.
❑ 1100-0600 Mon.-Sat., 2200-0600 Sun. U-Bahn 3-6 Odeonsplatz.
A good spot for night owls.

WEINSTUBE HOLZBAUER Frauenstrasse 10.
❑ 1630-0100 Mon.-Fri., 1100-1600 Sat. Closed hol. S-Bahn Isartor.
Munich's oldest Württemberg wine tavern has a wine garden in summer.

ROLANDSECK BADISCHE WEINSTUBE Viktoriastrasse 23.
❑ 0900-0100. U-Bahn 3 Bonner Platz.
This is a popular Schwabing (see **A-Z***) wine tavern offering the latest wines from Baden.*

Accidents & Breakdowns: In the event of a minor accident, follow the usual procedure of exchanging names, addresses and insurance details. If the accident is serious or someone has been injured, the police should be called immediately and you should take the names and addresses of any witnesses.

In the case of breakdowns contact either of the two main automobile clubs which operate a joint 24-hr breakdown service, the ADAC and the DTC (see **Driving**), using the emergency telephones placed at 10-km intervals along the autobahns (motorways), or alternatively, tel: 19211. Assistance is free but a charge is made for towing or spare parts. There are reciprocal agreements with the AA and the RAC so arrange for the appropriate documentation before leaving home. See **Consulates**, **Driving**, **Emergency Numbers**.

Accommodation: A complete list of hotels and pensions in Munich can be obtained from the German Tourist Office in London, Nightingale House, 65 Curzon St, tel: 071-4953990, and reservations in writing should be made well in advance. If, however, you arrive without a reservation, go to the *Fremdenverkehrsamt* (tourist office booking service) at the airport (see **A–Z**) or the Hauptbahnhof (see **Railways**) where accommodation will be arranged for you for a fee of DM 3 (see **Tourist Information**). The room price quoted to you includes taxes and services (and usually breakfast as well). Apart from hotels, the office will also assist you to book a room in a pension, which is simpler and cheaper than a hotel, a *Gasthaus* (inn) or a private house. See **Camping & Caravanning**, **Youth Hostels**.

Airport: Munich airport, 10 km east of the city at Riem, has daily connections to all the major German and European destinations. It offers all the usual facilities such as a post office, car-rental agencies (see **Car Hire**), tourist-information office (see **Accommodation**, **Tourist Information**), newsstands, a nursery, a left-luggage office, showers, snack bars, restaurants and souvenir shops. Transport to and from the airport includes a bus service with departures every 15 min (0600-2130) for the Hauptbahnhof (see **Railways**). The journey takes half an hour and costs DM 5.50 (DM 10 return). Night buses run according to flight schedules. You can also take the S-Bahn by catching bus 37 from the airport to Riem S-Bahn station, then taking line 6 which passes through the Hauptbahnhof. Alternatively take bus 91 to Max-Weber-Platz then U-Bahn line 4 or 5; or bus 38 to Trudering (Mon.-Fri.) then S-Bahn line 4. Taxis cost about DM 28 to the centre of town.

For general flight information, tel: 9211-2127.

Alte Peter: Climb the 303 steps to the top of the fondly named Old Peter tower of the Peterskirche (see **CHURCHES**, **WALK 2**, **A-Z**), with its eight clocks, and admire the view (1000-1700 Mon.-Sat.; DM 2).
U-Bahn 3, 6; S-Bahn Marienplatz.

Alte Pinakothek: This imposing, Venetian-style building houses paintings collected by the Wittelsbach family from the early 16thC onwards. Among the German masters on the first floor are two of Albrecht Dürer's (1471-1528) most famous paintings, his *Self-portrait* and the impressive *Four Apostles*. There is also a large collection of 17thC Dutch and Flemish paintings, dominated by Rubens' works. Early Italian artists – Botticelli, Raphael, Titian and Tintoretto – are also well represented. Particularly noteworthy, in one of the three rooms displaying the works of significant 17th-18thC French painters, are two paintings by Poussin, *Midas und Bacchus* and *Beweinung Christi*, and a *Sunrise* by Claude Lorrain. Venetian painters represented include Canaletto and Guardi, and Murillo and El Greco figure among the Spanish artists. The ground-floor collections include works by Hans Holbein the Elder and Pieter Brueghel the Elder. See **MUSEUMS 1**.

Alter Botanischer Garten: Munich's first botanical garden was laid out by Ludwig von Sckell in 1812 and became a public park between 1935-37. It boasts a grand neoclassical portal bearing a Latin inscription by Goethe and is dominated by a huge Neptune fountain by Joseph Wackerle. See **PARKS & GARDENS**.

Alter Hof: The first Munich residence of the Bavarian royal family and Germany's first emperor, Ludwig the Bavarian (a modern statue of the latter stands in front of the new portal on the north side). The original 13thC building was almost entirely altered in the early

19thC but, after suffering war damage in the 1940s, the Zwingerstock on the west side and the Burgstock on the south side of the courtyard were both reconstructed in their original form during the 1960s. The latter features the picturesque Affenturm (1470), or Monkey Tower, decorated with heraldic paintings. The tower on the south side dates from 1460 and dominates the attractive courtyard. See **BUILDINGS 1**, **WALK 2**.

Altes Hackerhaus: See **WALK 1**.

Altes Rathaus (Old Town Hall):
Built in 1470-80 by Jörg von Halsbach after the first town hall was destroyed by fire, its exterior was completely reconstructed after the last war following original plans. The restored Gothic banqueting hall, with its wooden barrel vault decorated with carved symbols and its painted frieze of coats of arms, is the most perfect example of its kind in Germany. It holds copies of Grasser's famous Morisco dancers, the originals of which can be seen in the Münchner Stadtmuseum (see **MUSEUMS 2**) – out of the initial 16, only ten have survived. The west gable is embellished with a modern statue of Ludwig the Bavarian, the east with one of Heinrich der Löwe, founder of Munich, while the passageway contains a memorial to the German soldiers who died in World War II. On the south side there is a statue of Juliet which was presented by Munich's twin city of Verona. The tower now houses the delightful Spielzeugmuseum (see **CHILDREN**) of Ivan Steiger, the caricaturist. See **BUILDINGS 2**, **WALKS 1 & 2**.

Altes Residenztheater (Cuvilliéstheater): This 18thC rococo theatre, designed by Court Architect Cuvilliés (see **A-Z**), is one of the loveliest buildings in Munich. The auditorium has four tiers of seats and is richly decorated in gold, white and red. The magnificent Electors' Box forms the focal point of the whole. If you want to attend an opera (mainly Mozart), play or concert here (dress is fairly formal), you must book up seven days in advance at the booking office, Maximilianstrasse 11 (1000-1300, 1530-1730 Mon.-Fri., 1000-1230 Sat.). The theatre is also open for viewing 1400-1700 Mon.-Sat., 1000-1700 Sun. & hol. (DM 2). U-Bahn 3-6 Odeonsplatz; S-Bahn Marienplatz.

Andechs: The late-14thC Benedictine abbey at Andechs was established on the site of a former 12thC fortress. The original 15thC Gothic church was given its baroque interior by Johann Baptist Zimmermann who created the stuccowork and wall and ceiling paintings (1751-55). Note the gilt wooden statue of the Virgin, dating from 1500, above the high altar. The abbey's famous brewery, which produces the popular Andechs beer, is still fully operational. See **EXCURSION 1**.

Asam Brothers: Egid Quirin (1692-1750) and Cosmas Damian Asam (1686-1739) were both practising architects who studied in Rome and were responsible for introducing a distinctive Bavarian form of Roman baroque to southern Germany. The former also specialized in stuccowork and sculpture, and the latter in fresco painting. Together they funded and collaborated on the decoration of the spectacular Sankt-Johann-Nepomuk-Kirche which stands next door to their house, the Asamhaus (see **BUILDINGS 2**, **WALK 1**, **A-Z**), in Sendlinger Strasse and which became known as the Asamkirche (see **CHURCHES**, **WALK 1**, **A-Z**).

Asamhaus: A four-storeyed house purchased in 1733 by Egid Quirin Asam (see **A-Z**) who proceeded to decorate it with rich baroque stuccowork. Note the mythological figures representing the arts and sciences, and Athena, the goddess of wisdom, pointing upwards to the classical heaven on the facade of the lower two floors. To the right you will also see the Christian heaven with the Virgin Mary, and on the left the sensual world with satyrs and fauns. See **BUILDINGS 2**, **WALK 1**.

Asamkirche (Sankt-Johann-Nepomuk-Kirche): Egid Quirin Asam (see **A-Z**), with his brother Cosmas Damian established and built this church dedicated to St. Johann Nepomuk between 1733 and 1746. Originally a private church attached to their house (see **Asamhaus**), the building constitutes a complete work of art in typical Asam style. The saint, with two angels, is featured above the portal. Inside, a balcony runs around the high, narrow interior which is lavishly decorated in the late-baroque manner to a quite overwhelming degree, with not one inch left uncovered. The dramatic high altar is crowned by a representation of God surrounded by angels holding Christ on the Cross, and there are numerous stucco reliefs depicting scenes from the saint's life as well as ceiling frescoes on the same theme. See **CHURCHES**, **WALK 1**.

Baby-sitters: The staff of the Babysitter-Service (tel: 229291) speak several languages and charge DM 8-15 per evening. Alternatively, enquire at your hotel reception desk. See CHILDREN, **Children**.

Bad Tölz: The attractive main street of this pretty town rises steeply from the river and is lined with traditional, painted houses. Formerly on the salt-trade route, Bad Tölz has a long history as an important market town, and the iodized springs discovered in 1845 gave it an additional economic boost as a spa. Visit the Kalvarienberg with its seven chapels.

The one at the top is dedicated to St. Leonard, a popular Bavarian and Austrian saint invoked as the deliverer of prisoners and guardian of horses. The saint's day (6 Nov.) is celebrated by the Leonardiritt, a procession of horse-drawn carts.

Banks: See **Currency, Money, Opening Times.**

Bayerischer Hof Hotel: See **Montgelas-Palais.**

Bayerisches Nationalmuseum: An art-history collection, housed in 47 rooms, which extends from late antiquity to the 19thC. The wide range of exhibits extends from jewellery to armour and altar pictures to tapestries, with a special emphasis on sculpture. There are also collections of porcelain, gold and silverware, clocks, musical instruments and folk art (rustic furniture, costumes, votive gifts and a series of Nativity scenes of great variety and individuality). See **MUSEUMS 1.**

Bayerisches Staatstheater am Gärtnerplatz: Originally built in late-neoclassical style (1864-65) as the Royal Folk Theatre in the reign of Ludwig II, this attractive building in its leafy square now stages light opera, ballet and musicals. If you want to see a performance, book in advance 1000-1300, 1530-1730 Mon.-Fri., 1000-1230 Sat. (dress fairly formal). U-Bahn 1, 2 Fraunhoferstrasse; tram 18, 20.

Benediktbeuern: Famous for its baroque monastery and church of St. Benedikt. The monastery, probably the oldest Benedictine house

north of the Alps, was where the *Carmina Burana* originated – goliard songs dating from medieval times. The present church dates from 1680-85 and is decorated with frescoes by Hans Georg Asam, father of the famous Asam brothers (see **A-Z**). Behind the chancel to the north is a separate chapel by Johann Michael Fischer, the Chapel of St. Anastasia. The ceiling paintings are by Johann Jakob Zeiller and the altar paintings by Jacopo Amigoni.

Best Buys: Bavarian specialities include tailored coats, jackets, etc. made from Loden cloth (a waterproof, traditionally green, wool fabric), and porcelain from Nymphenburg (see **NYMPHENBURG**, **Schloss Nymphenburg**). Traditional local costumes are also popular with visitors, including *tracht* for men (a fitted, grey jacket with a green collar), dirndl dresses with tight bodices for women, and the famous leather breeches known as lederhosen. Electrical goods and hi-fi equipment are also worth looking at as the Germans have an excellent reputation for precision and quality in this field. See **SHOPPING 1, 2, 3**, **Shopping**.

Bicycle & Motorcycle Hire: Cycling is one of the best ways of seeing the city. Bicycles can be hired from Lothar Borucki, Hans-Sachs-Strasse 7 (near Sendlinger-Tor-Platz); Radl Gipp, Kirchenstrasse 23 (Haidhausen); Fahradverleih, Zweibrückernstrasse 8; Bicycle Rental Englischer Garten (corner of Königinstrasse and Veterinärstrasse. Hire is available in summer Sat., Sun. & hol. only and is usually DM 18 per day, DM 90 per week). Motorcycles can also be hired from Fahradverleih (see above) at around DM 80 per day, DM 350-400 per week.

BMW-Museum: This unusual museum at Petuelring 130 presents the technical development of the car and motorcycle in particularly interesting ways. All in all it is far more than a mere display of this famous German firm's products. Also films, videos and slide shows in English. Open 0900-1700 (DM 4.50). U-Bahn 2, 3 Olympiazentrum.

Botanischer Garten: Laid out between 1909-14 on the initiative of the botanist Karl Goebel, the gardens cover an area of 20 ha. At the entrance, in front of the main building, is a delightful ornamental court decorated with majolica figures from the Nymphenburger Porzellan-manufaktur (see **NYMPHENBURG**) by Wackerle. To the right of the entrance are the hothouses containing 6000 different types of plants. Sections of the gardens are devoted to particular interests such as ecology, genetics, medicine and protected varieties. The rose garden with its café and the rhododendron grove are especially charming. Other attractions include the arboretum, the ornamental lake and the area containing plant life of different continents, including an extensive Alpine section. See **PARKS & GARDENS**.

Budget:

Hotel breakfast	DM 6-25.50
Dish of the Day	from DM 10
Beer/lager	from DM 3.70 (pint)
House wine	from DM 20 (bottle)
Brandy	from DM 3.80 (glass)

Bürgersaal: See **WALK 1**.

Buses: An extensive network of bus routes covers the entire city and its environs. Buses usually run till 0100 and the longest you will have to wait is 20 min. The Federal Railways also operate two bus networks: Bahnbus (for travel within Germany) and the German section of Europa-bus (with connections to around 200 cities in Europe). There is no bus station for these services but buses stop opposite Starnberg Station in Arnulfstrasse. For enquiries about specific destinations or connections, contact the travel centre in the Hauptbahnhof (see **Railways**). The Europabus booking office is in Starnberg Station. See **Transport**.

Cameras & Photography: There is no shortage of film, cameras and photographic equipment in Munich. The cost of a 36-exposure colour film is around DM 8-10. Most department stores offer good developing services and often have special offers.

Camping & Caravanning: The four main camp sites in the Munich area are Munich-Thalkirchen Camping Ground (municipal), Zentralländstrasse 49, 8 Munich 70, tel: 7231707 (about 5 km from the city centre, open mid Mar.-end Oct.); Camping Ground Nord-West, Dachauer Strasse 571, 8 Munich 50, tel: 1506936 (open all year); Camping Ground Langwieder See, Eschenrieder Strasse 119, 8 Munich 60, tel: 8141566 (8 km from Munich along the Stuttgart autobahn, open 1 April-mid Oct.).

Expect to pay around DM 4.90 per adult, DM 3-4.50 for a tent, DM 4 for a car, and DM 4.50-6 for a camper. For more details about official camp sites and costs, contact the Deutscher Camping Club, Mandlstrasse 28, D-8000 Munich 40, tel: 334021. Note also that there are specific road rules for caravanners (see **Driving**).

There is a sleeping tent for young people at Franz-Schrank-Strasse 8, Munich 19, tel: 1414300, which has 400 places, costs DM 6 per person and allows stays of up to three nights.

Car Hire: To hire a car in Germany you have to be over 18 years old and have held a valid licence for at least six months. If you pay by credit card, you won't have to leave a deposit (usually hefty). All the major international car-hire firms have offices in Munich, and most have branches at the airport (see **A-Z**) and the Hauptbahnhof (see **Railways**). Remember to ask about special weekend rates with unlimited mileage. If you prefer to go to a local agency, either look one up in the *Yellow Pages* or ask at your hotel reception desk. See **Driving**.

Chemists: Most chemists keep normal opening hours (see **Opening Times**) and also operate a rota system so that at least one shop is open at night and at weekends. Details are displayed in the window of every chemist, or you can phone the emergency chemist service on 594475 for information. You will have to pay a prescription charge for medicines obtained on a doctor's prescription, although you may be charged the full price for some painkillers, cough mixtures, etc. InterApotheke, on the corner of Luisenstrasse and Elisenstrasse near the north exit of the Hauptbahnhof (see **Railways**), stocks British and American products. See **Health**.

Chiemsee: Chiemsee, also known as 'the Bavarian Sea' because of its size, is Bavaria's largest lake. Its main attractions are the two islands of Fraueninsel (Ladies' Island) and Herreninsel (Lords' Island). The former houses a Benedictine monastery founded in the 8thC, and is dominated by the onion dome of the Church of St. Maria which contains valuable frescoes dating from 1160-70. Herreninsel is famous for Schloss Herrenchiemsee which was commissioned by Ludwig II in 1873 and was modelled on the Palace of Versailles. Work had to stop in 1886 when the king ran out of money. Nevertheless, his copy was well executed: particularly striking are the State Room, the magnificent Hall of Mirrors and the attractive French Gardens.

Children: There are plenty of outdoor pursuits for children in and around Munich but one of the main sources of endless fun for all ages is the city's parks. In addition to the various playgrounds in the Englischer Garten (see **A-Z**) there are also rowing boats and paddle boats for hire on the lake in summer; the Chinese Tower beer garden with its delightful historic roundabout; and a steam-powered roundabout at the Seegarten beer garden. The Westpark has two elaborate adventure playgrounds and the Olympiapark (see **A-Z**) also has one, as well as a lake with rowing boats. In winter, children can toboggan on the hills there. See **PARKS & GARDENS**.
For the more literary-minded, there is an International Youth Library at Schloss Blutenburg (see **BUILDINGS 1**, **A-Z**) which contains books in 12 languages. They also run a children's programme of discussions, films and performances. See **CHILDREN**, **Baby-sitters**.

Cinemas: Europa Filmtheater, Atlantik Palast, Schwanthalerstrasse 4, shows English-language films and the latest blockbusters. U-Bahn 4, 5; S-Bahn Karlsplatz.
Cinema, Nymphenburger Strasse 31 shows a variety of films including

older classics, some with the original soundtrack and some dubbed. U-Bahn 1 Stiglmaierplatz.

City Fortifications: Only three gates now remain of the original five city gates which survived until 1800 from the early-14thC fortifications of Munich constructed by the Emperor, Ludwig the Bavarian.

Sendlinger Tor – the main high tower in the middle was demolished at the beginning of the 19thC. The two hexagonal side towers and the walls were restored in 1860 by Zenetti. In 1906 the three arches were replaced by a single large arch. See **WALK 1**.

Isartor – The main tower was built in 1337 and the two octagonal side towers between 1429-99. The fresco on the front depicts Ludwig the Bavarian's triumph after the Battle of Ampfing (1332). Today the southern tower houses the Valentin-Musäum (see **A–Z**). See **WALK 2**.

Karlstor – the city's western gate consists of medieval towers reconstructed in 1791. See **WALK 1**, **Karlsplatz**.

Climate: Munich enjoys a central-continental climate: warmish summers with an average temperature of 23°C, and cold winters.

Complaints: If you have been overcharged, or find that prices do not correspond to those displayed, ask to see the owner or manager of the premises. If you are still not satisfied, then you can report the establishment to the *Fremdenverkehrsamt*, the central tourist office (see

Tourist Information). They have no legal force but they will investigate any problem.

Consulates:
UK – Amalienstrasse 62, tel: 394015/19.
R. of Ireland – Mauerkircherstrasse 1a, tel: 985723/25.
Canada – Tal 29/III, tel: 222661.
USA – Königinstrasse 5, tel: 23011.

Conversion Chart:

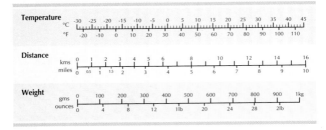

Credit Cards: See **Money.**

Crime & Theft: Although Munich does not have a reputation as a dangerous city, the usual precautions should be taken. Don't carry your wallet in your back pocket or hang your handbag over the back of your chair in a restaurant, don't leave valuables exposed in a parked car, and do keep a separate list of the numbers of your traveller's cheques along with a note of your passport number. If you are the victim of a theft go straight to the police who will give you a copy of their report which you will need for any insurance claim. A lost passport should also be reported to your consulate and lost traveller's cheques to the issuing office. See **Consulates, Emergency Numbers, Insurance, Police.**

Currency: The Deutsche Mark (DM) is the German monetary unit. It is divided into 100 Pfennig (Pf). Coins in circulation are worth 1, 2, 5, 10 and 50 Pf, and DM 1, 2, 5 and 10. Notes are in denominations of DM 5, 10, 20, 50, 100, 500 and 1000. See **Money**.

Customs Allowances:

Duty Paid Into:	Cigarettes	*or*	Cigars	*or*	Tobacco	Spirits	Wine
E C	300		75		400 g	1.5 *l*	5 *l*
U K	300		75		400 g	1.5 *l*	5 *l*

Cuvilliés, Francois de, the Elder (1695-1768): The architect and interior decorator responsible for some of the finest rococo buildings in southern Germany came from what was then Austria, and began his career in Munich as Duke Maximilian Emanuel's Court Dwarf before he became Court Architect in 1725. His most famous works include the Theatinerkirche facade (see **CHURCHES, WALK 3**) and the Altes Residenztheater (see **A-Z**). See **WALKS 2 & 3**.

Cuvilliéstheater: See Altes Residenztheater.

Dachau: 17 km northwest of Munich. This attractive old town is dominated by the remains of a baroque castle situated in a pleasant park, with a terrace looking out over the town and the surrounding countryside. The castle was originally built for Dukes Wilhelm IV and Albrecht V in the 16thC and was rebuilt by Joseph Effner (see **A-Z**) in 1715. The only surviving section houses an elegant café.
The site of the notorious concentration camp established by Heinrich Himmler in 1933 on the edge of town (Alte Römerstrasse) became a memorial to the dead in 1965. The museum now there documents the

atrocities at the camp and there is a film in English at 1130 and 1530.
You can also visit two reconstructed prison barracks (0900-1700 Tue.-
Sun.; free). Call the Dachau tourist office on 08131-84566 for further
information.

Dentists: See Health.

Deutsches Jagd- und Fischereimuseum: The German Hunting
and Fishing Museum is housed in a former church at Neuhauser Strasse
53. Displays include large dioramas of animals, hunting weapons, and
paintings and drawings. Open 0930-1700 (also 1900-2200 Mon.), costs
DM 4. U-Bahn 3, 6; S-Bahn Marienplatz. See **WALK 1**.

Deutsches Museum: An impressive museum tracing the development of science, technology and industry up to the present day. There
is a full-scale mine, vintage cars, ships and planes, musical instruments,
exhibits on space travel, and a new microelectronics section.
Increasingly, displays are labelled in English as well as German. See
MUSEUMS 2.

Deutsches Theatermuseum: This theatre museum at Galeriestrasse 4a contains over four million documents from the history of world theatre, including sketches of stage designs, props and costumes, libretti, etc. and a large Wagner collection (1000-1600 Tue.-Thu., 1000-1430 Fri., closed hol.; free). U-Bahn 3-6 Odeonsplatz.

Diessen: See EXCURSION 1.

Disabled People: The installation of lifts in all U-Bahn stations is gradually taking place and wheelchair travel is now possible at least in the central area of the city. The Nationaltheater (see **A-Z**), the Herkulessaal (see **Music**) and the Gasteig (see **A-Z**) are all accessible by wheelchair. There is a toilet for disabled people at Sendlinger Tor (see **City Fortifications**), and public places, such as museums and restaurants are gradually becoming aware of the need to provide similar facilities. Ask for full details at the Karlsplatz municipal information centre where you can obtain the *Stadtführer für Behinderte* (*Town Guide for the Disabled*) and the special MVV map of the Munich transportation system indicating all the U-Bahn stations with lifts and toilets for the disabled.
The standard map of Munich published by Falk (*Falkplan*) has now been reissued, marked with all the facilities for the disabled. Wheelchairs are available at the airport (see **A-Z**), Hellabrunn Zoo (see **CHILDREN**), and from Medizinisches Fachhaus von Schlieben, Sonnenstrasse 7; tel: 555295 (DM 35 per week, DM 250 deposit). See **Health**, **Insurance**.

Dreifaltigkeitskirche: See CHURCHES.

Drinks: The principal drink in Munich is, of course, beer, and it comes in all strengths, colours and tastes. Bavarian beer, such as the lager-style beer called *Helles*, tends to be lighter on the whole than other German brews, so if you want a dark beer ask for *Dunkles*. Other types include the strong *Starkbier* (the best-known brand being Salvator), *Maibock* (brewed in May), *Weissbier* (light, fizzy beer) and the famous *Wiesenbier* brewed for the Oktoberfest (see **A-Z**). As well as

these, there are the internationally-known brands such as Löwenbräu, Spatenbräu, Pils and Bock. It is normal for everyone to drink beer by the litre glass (*Mass*) in beer gardens or beer cellars, but in restaurants you will normally be served a half litre. See **BEER CELLARS**.

Despite the emphasis on beer it shouldn't be forgotten that Munich has some fine wines on offer, mainly from the Rhine Valley (in brown bottles) and the Moselle region (in green bottles). Names such as Liebfraumilch and Oppenheimer are already familiar ones abroad, but you should also try Schloss Johannisberger, Rüdesheimer, Bernkasteler and Piesporter, all of which possess excellent reputations. The sparkling wine known as *Sekt* is also very palatable. See **WINE TAVERNS**.

Non-alcoholic drinks include bottled mineral waters, a wide range of fruit juices, such as grape, apple, and blackcurrant or redcurrant, and the usual selection of soft drinks.

Driving: If you are planning to take your car into Germany you must have a driving licence, car logbook, third-party insurance, warning triangle, first-aid kit and car nationality sticker. Seat belts must be worn in the front seats and, if the car is fitted with them, in the back as well. Although the German road network is excellent, traffic jams are quite common. The speed limits are 50 kph in built-up areas, 100 kph on main roads and unlimited speeds on autobahns (motorways), although the suggested maximum is 130 kph. Unlimited speeds on autobahns are possible mainly because German drivers' lane discipline is excellent, and you must ensure that yours is also to avoid causing an accident. Vehicles pulling caravans should not exceed 80 kph. Keep a look out for any speed-limit signs, as police radar controls are frequent and you may have to pay an on-the-spot fine. The maximum blood/alcohol content is 0.8% and it is considered a serious offence to be over the limit.

The two main national automobile clubs are the Allgemeiner Deutscher Automobil-Club (ADAC), Am Westpark 8, D-8000 Munich 70, tel: 76760, and the Deutscher Touring Automobil Club (DTC), Amalienburgstrasse 23, Munich 60, tel: 8111048. See **Accidents & Breakdowns**, **Car Hire**, **Insurance**, **Parking**, **Petrol**, **Transport**.

Drugs: All drugs are illegal and there are severe penalties for offenders. Contact your embassy or consulate (see **A-Z**) if you are arrested for a drugs-related offence.

Eating Out: Munich is lucky enough to have many high-quality restaurants and in fact has the honour of being the only European city to have two three-star restaurants (Aubergine and Tantris – see **RESTAURANTS 1**). Establishments range from those offering de luxe German, French and international cuisine through to simpler, local eateries serving traditional Bavarian dishes, and places serving more ethnic foods, often to cater for those communities. These three categories are covered in the **RESTAURANTS** pages in the first half of the book. You can also try a *Gaststätte* or *Bräuhaus* (see **BEER CELLARS**) for down-to-earth cooking washed down by a beer, or one of the *Weinstuben* (see **WINE TAVERNS**) where wine is sold by the carafe or glass and there is usually a buffet. As well as these there is a wide choice of *Imbiss-Stuben* (snack bars) serving

tasty dishes. Price categories in the **RESTAURANTS** pages are based on a two-course meal without wine for one and are as follows:

Expensive:	over DM 50
Moderate:	DM 20-50
Inexpensive:	under DM 20

See **RESTAURANTS 1, 2, 3**, **Food**.

Effner, Joseph (1687-1745): Cuvilliés' (see **A-Z**) predecessor as Court Architect, a post he held from 1715, was a native of the nearby town of Dachau (see **A-Z**) and, like Cuvilliés, he trained in Paris. His major works include the Preysing-Palais (see **BUILDINGS 1**), the enlargement of Schloss Nymphenburg (see **BUILDINGS 1, NYMPHENBURG, A-Z**) and the Badenburg, Pagodenburg and Magdalenenklause in Nymphenburg Park (see **NYMPHENBURG**).

Electricity: 220-250 volts and 50-cycle AC. Small, two-pin plugs are used, for which UK appliances need an adaptor. These can be obtained from any airport shop.

Emergency Numbers:

Police	110
Fire	112
Ambulance	19222
Emergency medical aid	558651

Englischer Garten: The English Garden began life, in 1789, as a military park intended for the enjoyment of both military and public. Landscaped by the American Benjamin Thompson (Count von Rumford) in an English naturalistic manner with hills and vales and streams, it was gradually expanded and now begins at Prinzregentenstrasse in the city centre and extends north to Freimann before dwindling to a strip of green on either side of the River Isar. One of its main features is the Kleinhesseloher See, an artificial lake where you can boat in summer and skate in winter, as well as taking some refreshment at the popular beer garden and restaurant complex on the

east shore. The park's other popular beer gardens include the Chinese Tower to the south, with its wooden pagoda and weekend brass bands, horse-drawn carriage rides and roundabout, and the Aumeister to the north. You can climb up to the hill-top Monopteros – a small Ionic temple – from where there is a delightful view of the old city's spires. See **PARKS & GARDENS**, **Children**.

Ettal: The Benedictine monastery for which Ettal is famous was founded by Emperor Ludwig IV in 1330. The Gothic church, completed in 1370, possesses unique, twelve-sided, polygonal foundations and acquired a baroque facade with two towers and a chancel by Enrico Zuccalli in the 18thC. The rococo cupola is by Josef Schmuzer and the frescoes decorating it by Johann-Jakob Zeiller. The church also features stuccowork by J. B. Zimmermann and sculptures by Straub (see **A-Z**). See **EXCURSION 2**.

Events:
7 January-Shrove Tuesday: Fasching (Shrovetide Carnival), with masked processions and balls.
Spring: Starkbierfest (Strong Beer Festival) at the Salvator-Keller (see **BEER CELLARS**).
June: The beginning of summer cultural festivities, including the Nymphenburg Festival and concerts at Schleissheim Palace (see **Schleissheim**) and the Residenz (see **A-Z**).
Mid July-early August: Opernfestspiele (Opera Festival). See **Music**.
Mid September-first Sunday in October: Oktoberfest (see **A-Z**) on the Theresienwiese, 16 days of beer drinking, eating and fun.
December: Christkindlmarkt (Christmas Fair) in Marienplatz.

Feldherrnhalle: Completed in 1844 by F. von Gärtner, the Military Commanders' Hall is modelled on Florence's Loggia dei Lanzi and was erected in honour of the two great Bavarian generals, Tilly (1559-1632) and Wrede (1767-1838). Their statues, by Ludwig Schwanthaler, stand in the arcades and there is a monument on the back wall by F. von Miller to commemorate the heroic feats of the Bavarian army during the Franco-Prussian War. See **BUILDINGS 2, WALK 3**.

Food: One can eat very well indeed in Munich. There is a great variety of foods, from traditional Bavarian fare to all kinds of ethnic cuisines. Traditionally, however, one starts with soup, and some of the most typical are *Leberknödelsuppe* (potato and liver dumplings), *Linsensuppe* (lentils and sausage) and *Kartoffelsuppe* (potatoes, celery, leeks and parsnips). Favourite main courses usually include roast pork or veal. *Tellerfleisch* (boiled beef) with grated horseradish is also a popular dish, as is the famous *Leberkäs* (meat loaf)

which is often served cold as a snack. A wide variety of game, often served with interesting sauces, also appears on Munich menus during the appropriate seasons. Accompaniments often include a plain green or potato salad, sautéed potatoes, sauerkraut (white cabbage cooked in white wine and spices) or red cabbage cooked with apples and vinegar. Heading the list on the dessert side is Viennese *Apfelstrudel*, a great favourite in Munich, followed by cakes made with fruit, such as *Apfelkücherl* (apple) or *Zwetschgendatschi* (plum). There is also usually a huge choice of mouthwatering pastries and tarts.

In addition, Bavarians have a whole host of snacks designed to accompany the great quantities of beer they consume. Pork and veal with various combinations of spices and flavourings constitute the main ingredients of *Weisswürste* (white sausage). Try *Blutwurst* (black pudding) or grilled *Bratwurst* which are also very tasty. Fish brochettes are popular during the beer festivals, as are dishes of sliced radish.
See **RESTAURANTS 1, 2, 3, Eating Out**.

Frauenkirche: The twin towers of this massive, late-Gothic, brick edifice constitute Munich's most famous landmark (panoramic views of the city are to be had from the south tower which can be ascended by lift). Begun in 1468 by Jörg von Halspach, the cathedral was completed 20 years later. The vast interior with its eleven pairs of octagonal pillars was reconstructed after World War II, when the building suffered severe bomb damage, and it now appears disproportionately light and new in comparison to the exterior. Among the surviving original features are the central choir window by Peter Hemmel von Andlau (1493) and the windows to the right of the choir. Other attractions include the carved wooden

reliefs depicting scenes from the life of the Virgin Mary by Ignaz Günther (1774), the memorial tomb of Emperor Ludwig the Bavarian, the silver gilt shrine of St. Benno, patron saint of Bavaria, in the Benno Chapel (1601) and the wooden statue of St. Christopher at the entrance (c.1525). The crypt is the oldest burial place of the Wittelsbach family. See **CHURCHES**.

Garmisch-Partenkirchen: 85 km from Munich. Garmisch-Partenkirchen is an attractive town and popular winter-sports centre set in a broad valley dominated by the Zugspitze (the highest mountain in Germany at 2966 m) in the Wetterstein mountains. For a panoramic view of the whole chain take the cable car up the Wank (90-min return trip) or, if you have a little more time, ascend the Zugspitze on the rack-and-pinion railway (Zugspitzbahn) from behind the main Garmisch station (every half hour; DM 43 return for a half-day excursion). It is also possible to visit the Olympic ski stadium and the Partnachklamm, a beautiful gorge. Day trip by train including ascent of Zugspitze: DM 62, without ascent of Zugspitze: DM 26 (trains every hour).

Gasteig: This massive new cultural centre, at Rosenheimerstrasse 5, with its stark brick-and-glass facade (making it much less attractive outside than in) was completed in 1985. The purpose-built concert hall, the Philharmonie, is home to the excellent Munich Philharmonic Orchestra. Tickets for their concerts, and for visiting orchestras and musicians, are available two to four weeks in advance. Chamber orchestra concerts and dramas are staged in the smaller Carl-Orff Saal, and the Kleiner Konzertsaal also specializes in performances of chamber music, often free, performed by the students of the Richard Strauss Conservatory housed in the same building. In addition, the Gasteig has its own small theatre, the Black Box, which is often used by visiting drama companies, and quite regularly has performances in English, as well as being a concert venue. Bookings: 1030-1400, 1500-1800 Mon.-Fri.,1030-1400 Sat. S-Bahn Rosenheimer Platz.

Glockenspiel: Munich's famous carillon of 43 bells in the tower of the Neues Rathaus (see **BUILDINGS 2**, **A-Z**) plays a variety of folk tunes

for eight minutes to which delightful, larger-than-life, painted wooden figures move. First of all is a scene from the wedding celebrations of Wilhelm V and Renata von Lothringen (1568): a tournament which the couple view from their royal box. Next, a circle of coopers go through the motions of a traditional dance which originally celebrated the end of the plague of 1517 and is still performed every seven years during the Fasching (see **Events**). Finally, when everything seems to have come to an end, the golden cockerel perched above the entire scene flaps his wings and can just be heard to crow above the din of the city. Performances 1100 daily, also 1200 and 1700 (May-Oct.). A second Glockenspiel featuring the Münchner Kindl (Child of Munich), a nightwatchman and an angel takes place at 2100. See **WALK 1**.

Hauptmünzamt: This Renaissance building was constructed by Wilhelm Egkl (1563-67) for Duke Albrecht V as his stables and library, and to contain his growing art collection. Its later civic function as the Bavarian Mint lasted until 1983 when it became the Office for the Preservation of Historic Monuments. All that remains of the original structure is the Italianate arcaded courtyard surrounded by covered balconies on three floors. See **BUILDINGS 2, WALK 2**.

Hauptpost: See **BUILDINGS 1, WALK 3, Palais Törring-Jettenbach**.

Health: Citizens of EC countries are entitled to free medical and dental treatment throughout their stay in Germany. You should obtain an E 111 from your local DSS office before you leave home, and present this to the nearest sickness-insurance office (Allgemeine Ortskrankenkassen or AOK) in Munich. They will give you an entitlement certificate and indicate which doctors and dentists are in the scheme. If you fail to get an entitlement certificate before seeking treatment, give the doctor your E 111 when you pay the fee and you will be refunded later (you have ten days in which to arrange this). If hospital treatment is required it must be passed by the AOK first (except in emergency cases). You can get a list of English-speaking doctors and dentists from your consulate (see **A-Z**). See **Chemists**, **Disabled People**, **Emergency Numbers**, **Insurance**.

Heiliggeistkirche: The 14thC Gothic Church of the Holy Ghost at Tal 77 has been extensively rebuilt and remodelled several times in various styles: the facade is 19thC neo-baroque, while the choir buttresses and north wall of the nave are Gothic. The interior rococo stuccowork and frescoes are by the Asam brothers (see **A-Z**). The Marienaltar boasts a magnificent 15thC wooden sculpture, the *Hammerthaler Madonna*, and there are figures of angels by J. G. Greiff flanking the high altar by Nikolas Stuber. U-Bahn 3, 6; S-Bahn Marienplatz. See **WALK 2**.

Hellabrunn Zoo: See **CHILDREN**.

Hirschgarten: Dates from 1720 and has been used variously for raising game, growing hops, as a mulberry plantation and as a zoo. In the 1950s and '60s it was greatly extended, and today contains a deer enclosure and a protected area containing oak trees up to 150 years old. See **PARKS & GARDENS**.

Hofbräuhaus: See **BEER CELLARS**, **WALK 2**.

Hofgarten: The Renaissance Court Garden dates from Duke Maximilian I's time (1613-17) and features a central temple crowned by a domed roof with a copy of a bronze figure symbolizing Bavaria. Paths lined with ornamental flower beds radiate from this focal point and open into circular areas with fountains and seats. The Residenz (see **BUILDINGS 1**, **MUSEUMS 2**, **WALK 3**, **A-Z**) stands to the south, to the west and north are arcades, and the gaunt remains of the former Armeemuseum (Army Museum) lies to the east. See **PARKS & GARDENS**.

Hohenschwangau: See EXCURSION 2.

Insurance: You should take out travel insurance covering you against medical expenses, theft, and loss of property and money, for the duration of your stay. Your travel agent can recommend a suitable policy. See **Crime & Theft**, **Disabled People**, **Driving**, **Health**, **Lost Property**.

Isartor: See **City Fortifications**.

Karlsplatz: The square was originally laid out in 1791 around the Karlstor (see **City Fortifications**) and named after the unpopular Elector Karl Theodor, but is now popularly known as the Stachus (after an inn called Wirtschaft zum Stachus which once stood on the site of the department store Kaufhof). The front towers of the original gate were rebuilt and later incorporated into the semicircle of buildings surrounding the square, a favourite gathering place in the summer, with its large fountain (see **WALK 1**). Because of heavy traffic, a subway has been built allowing pedestrians to cross the busy square by an underground route which also contains a shopping centre. The pedestrian precinct begins in Neuhauser Strasse behind the Karlstor. The massive 19thC Palace of Justice stands opposite the Karlstor on the other side of the busy Sonnenstrasse. U-Bahn 3-6; S-Bahn Karlsplatz.

Königsplatz: Originally conceived by Ludwig I with his architect Leo von Klenze as a place of culture and the site of architectural monuments to history, this rather overwhelming square, with its powerful neoclassical buildings, was designed by Karl von Fischer in 1811. During the Nazi era it was frequently the scene of mass rallies. The north side is dominated by Klenze's 'Ionic' Glyptothek (see **MUSEUMS 2**) and the west side by his 'Doric' Propyläen (see **BUILDINGS 2**). The exhibition building to the south of the square, now housing the Staatliche Antikensammlung (see **A-Z**), was built by Georg Friedrich Ziebland and is fronted by eight Corinthian columns with pediment sculptures by Schwanthaler. U-Bahn 2 Königsplatz. See **WALK 3**.

Landsberg am Lech: The main attraction in this medieval fortress town which rises in tiers above the Lech valley, is the triangular town square, the Marktplatz, with its fountain and brightly coloured houses. Dominikus Zimmermann, the architect Bürgomeister of Landsberg who built the Wieskirche (see **A-Z**) was also responsible for the stunning 18thC facade of the town hall. The 14thC Schmalztor (Beautiful Tower) stands at the corner of the square. The steep Alte Bergstrasse leads to the Bayertor (Bavarian Gate) which dates from 1425 and is one of the best-preserved gates in Germany. Hitler was once imprisoned in the fortress where he wrote *Mein Kampf*. See **EXCURSION 1**.

Laundries: Munich has numerous coin-operated launderettes (*Wäscherei*) where you can do your own washing at a fraction of the price you would be charged in a hotel (DM 6-7 per 5 kg load, DM 0.5-1 for drying). You will find launderettes at Pestalozzistrasse 16 (near

Sendlinger-Tor-Platz); Lilienstrasse 73 (near the Deutsches Museum);
Klenzestrasse 18 (near Gärtnerplatz); Belgradstrasse 11a (Schwabing);
and Landshuter Allee 77 (near Rotkreuzplatz, open 24 hr).

Lenbachhaus: Munich residence of the portrait painter Franz von
Lenbach who built it in collaboration with architect Gabriel von Seidl
from 1887-91. The villa is in Renaissance Florentine style, with
baroque details and a neoclassical entrance, and houses the Städtische
Galerie im Lenbachhaus (see **MUSEUMS 1**). See **BUILDINGS 2**, **WALK 3**.

Leopoldstrasse: Runs north of Ludwigstrasse through Schwabing
(see **A-Z**) into the suburban residential districts of the city. The most
interesting section of this famous street runs between Giselastrasse and
Münchener Freiheit, where its broad pavements are lined with poplar
trees, and café and restaurant tables in summer. Craftspeople, from sil-
houette-cutters to potters, offer their wares to the throngs of passers-by.

Lost Property: The city lost property office is at Rupperstrasse 19,
tel: 2331. There is also an office in the Hauptbahnhof (see **Railways**)
near platform 26, tel: 1286664. For objects lost at the airport (see **A-Z**),
tel: 9212263. See **Insurance**.

Löwenturm: See **WALK 2**.

Ludwigskirche: See **CHURCHES**.

Ludwigstrasse: Starts at Odeonsplatz (see **A-Z**) and continues north
into Schwabing (see **A-Z**), ending at the Siegestor (see **A-Z**). This grand
boulevard was designed for King Ludwig I who wanted to transform Munich
into a neoclassical city – a new Athens. The southern end,
from the palaces of Odeonsplatz, is mainly the work of Leo von Klenze.
An example of his neoclassical style can be seen in the old Ministry of
War building (1824-30) at No. 14, now the Bavarian State Archives,
which resembles a Florentine *palazzo*. From this point on the road was
completed by Klenze's successor, Court Architect Friedrich von
Gärtner.

Leopoldstrasse

Luitpoldpark: Originally a grove of 90 lime trees around a lawn with an obelisk, this attractive park today comprises 33 ha of lawns, rosebeds and massive trees. Bamberger Haus (1912) lies at the park's edge at Brunnerstrasse 2 and now houses a café and restaurant. See **PARKS & GARDENS**.

Marienplatz: The former site of a grain market, this historic square forms the heart of the city and contains both the Altes and the Neues Rathaus (see **BUILDINGS 2**, **A-Z**), the Mariensäule (see **A-Z**) and the Fischbrunnen (Fish Fountain). Now a pedestrian precinct, the square has

become a popular meeting place where street performers entertain and where occasionally there are more formal events such as performances of *Carmina Burana*. It is also the venue of an open-air party held at the end of Fasching (see **Events**) and the site of the Christkindlmarkt (see **Events**). U-Bahn 3, 6; S-Bahn Marienplatz. See **WALK 1**.

Mariensäule: The Column of the Virgin in Marienplatz (see **A–Z**) was erected by Maximilian I in 1632 to celebrate the city's preservation during the Swedish occupation. The base is decorated with allegorical figures representing plague, famine, war and heresy. The figure of the Virgin holding a sceptre, orb and the Christ child crowns the column.

Maximilianeum: The seat of the Bavarian Government dominates the east bank of the River Isar. It was built by Friedrich Bürklein and Gottfried Semper (1857-74) and was originally intended to be both an institute of higher education for gifted applicants to the civil services, and a picture gallery. The central portion of the building, decorated with mosaics on a gold background, is flanked by two wings of open arcades culminating in three-storeyed towers. Of the original interior decorations, only the frescoes in the conference room remain. See **BUILDINGS 2, WALK 2**.

Max-Joseph-Platz: A grand, sober square with a circular cobbled centre in the middle of which sits the bronze throned statue of the first king of Bavaria, Max I Joseph. The pedestal of the monument (unveiled in 1830) is decorated with allegorical figures and reliefs depicting the King's achievements. The square was laid out in its present form by the mid-19thC. The north side is bounded by the Königsbau of the

Residenz (see **BUILDINGS 1, MUSEUMS 2, A-Z**) and the west by the Residenzstrasse with its fine town houses. To the south are the arcades of the Main Post Office, the former Palais Törring-Jettenbach (see **BUILDINGS 1, A-Z**), to the east the beginning of Maximilianstrasse. U-Bahn 3-6 Odeonsplatz; S-Bahn Marienplatz. See **WALK 3**.

Michaelskirche: This large Renaissance church was built by Duke Wilhelm the Pious between 1583-97 for the city's Jesuits. The high, gabled facade is graced with the figures of dukes and electors of Bavaria and a bronze statue of Archangel Michael's triumph over Satan.

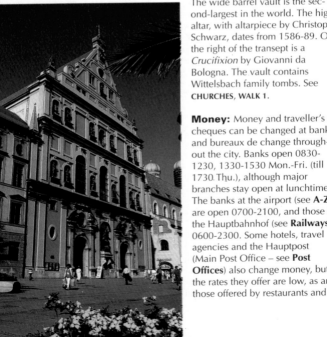

The wide barrel vault is the second-largest in the world. The high altar, with altarpiece by Christoph Schwarz, dates from 1586-89. On the right of the transept is a *Crucifixion* by Giovanni da Bologna. The vault contains Wittelsbach family tombs. See **CHURCHES, WALK 1**.

Money: Money and traveller's cheques can be changed at banks and bureaux de change throughout the city. Banks open 0830-1230, 1330-1530 Mon.-Fri. (till 1730 Thu.), although major branches stay open at lunchtime. The banks at the airport (see **A-Z**) are open 0700-2100, and those at the Hauptbahnhof (see **Railways**) 0600-2300. Some hotels, travel agencies and the Hauptpost (Main Post Office – see **Post Offices**) also change money, but the rates they offer are low, as are those offered by restaurants and shops which accept traveller's cheques. American dollars, Austrian schillings, Italian lire and Swiss francs can be changed at the 24-hr automatic change machine outside the Stadtsparkasse bank, Sparkassenstrasse 2, Tal. Eurocheques and all major credit cards are widely accepted as payment. The American Express office is at Promenadeplatz 6, tel: 21990. See **Crime & Theft**, **Currency**.

Montgelas-Palais: This elegant neoclassical palace at Promenadeplatz 2, with its Empire banqueting halls, was built for Count Maximilian Joseph von Montgelas by Herigoyen from 1811-13. It now forms part of the first-class Bayerischer Hof Hotel. U-Bahn 3-6 Odeonsplatz; S-Bahn Marienplatz; tram 19. See **WALK 3**.

Münchner Stadtmuseum: One of the main exhibits in this museum devoted to the history of Munich and Bavaria is Erasmus Grasser's famous 15thC Morisco (morris) dancers which he carved for the ball-

room of the Altes Rathaus (see **BUILDINGS 2**, **WALKS 1 & 2**, **A-Z**) where there are still copies. There are historic rooms from the 17th-20thC and separate areas covering photography, brewing, furnishings, musical instruments and puppets, making this a fascinating museum for everyone. There is also a film museum with daily showings of films, including English and American films. See **MUSEUMS 2**, **WALK 2**.

Music: The most important event in Munich's cultural calendar is the annual Opernfestspiele (Opera Festival – see **Events**), the grandest performances of which are given in the Nationaltheater (see **A-Z**). The prestigious Munich Philharmonic Orchestra is based in the Gasteig (see **A-Z**) and the city boasts many other fine music venues, including the Herkulessaal, Residenz, Residenzstrasse 1 (see **Residenz**) and the Musikhochschule, Arcisstrasse 12, where there are also free concerts by the students. Concerts may also take place in churches. Full details of these, and other events, are published in the *Münchner Monatsprogram* (see **What's On**). Open-air concerts

are held in summer in the Brunnenhof of the Residenz, and there is brass-band music at the Chinese pagoda in the Englischer Garten (see **PARKS & GARDENS**, **A-Z**). Jazz can be heard in small bars and clubs throughout Schwabing (see **A-Z**) and at the Kongressaal Deutsches Museum, Isarinsel. An annual international jazz festival is held in the Olympiapark (see **A-Z**), where rock and pop concerts also take place in the Olympiahalle.

Nationaltheater (Bayerische Staatsoper): Munich's magnificent neoclassical opera house on the Max-Joseph-Platz (see **A-Z**) was built from 1811-18 by Karl von Fischer and reconstructed by Leo von Klenze after a fire in 1823. In 1963 it was again rebuilt after being destroyed in the last war. The auditorium with its five balconies, royal box and magnificent chandelier is stunningly decorated in red, white and gold. The theatre has opera (with a festival, the Opernfestspiele – see

Events) and ballet seasons. If you want to see a performance, book up seven days in advance at Maximilianstrasse 11 (1000-1300, 1530-1730 Mon.-Fri., 1000-1230 Sat.). There are also guided tours 1400 Fri., costing DM 5. U-Bahn 3-6 Odeonsplatz; S-Bahn Marienplatz. See **WALK 3**.

Neue Pinakothek: This attractive postmodern building was completed in 1981 to house the collection of European art begun by Ludwig I. The collection, the main strength of which is 19thC European paintings, includes the work of French and German romantic painters Stieler, Schwind, Corot and Spitzweg. Other artists represented are Leibl (the 'modern Holbein'), French impressionists Manet and Cézanne, Van Gogh, Gauguin, Klimt and Schiele. See **MUSEUMS 1**.

Neue Sammlung: The 'New Collection' traces the history of design from the end of the 18thC to the present day and comprises over 22,000 objects, including textiles, ceramics, furniture and consumer items. It is officially known as the Museum für angewandte Kunst (Museum of Applied Art) and is in the National Museum, Prinzregentenstrasse 3 (1000-1700 Tue.-Sun. for specific exhibitions). Tram 20, bus 53, 55.

Neues Rathaus: This neo-Gothic edifice dominating the entire north side of the Marienplatz (see **A-Z**) has more affinity with a cathedral than a town hall. It was built by Georg Hauberrisser (1867-1908) in three stages. The main facade is richly decorated with statues of Bavarian kings, electors and princes of the Wittelsbach family, allegorical figures, animals, masks and coats of arms. There are six inner courtyards, including the dramatic ceremonial courtyard with its tower and spiral staircase. The 85-m-high tower housing the Glockenspiel (see

A-Z) is crowned with the symbolic figure of the Münchner Kindl (Child of Munich). See **BUILDINGS 2**, **WALK 1**.

Neuschwanstein: See EXCURSION 2.

Newspapers: English newspapers can be bought at International Presse in the Hauptbahnhof (see **Railways**), in the Karlsplatz and at larger newsstands and hotels. Anglia Bookshop, Schellingstrasse 3 also carries a good selection. *The Financial Times* and *The Guardian* are published in Frankfurt and so are widely available. See **What's On**.

Nightlife: Although there are bars, discos and music venues in the city centre, the real centre of nightlife in Munich is Schwabing (see **A-Z**), particularly the area east of Leopoldstrasse, with many discos and bars along Occamstrasse. There are also student pubs and music venues in the Türkenstrasse area. Most pubs close at 0100 although a number have extended hours. See **BARS**, **BEER CELLARS**, **NIGHTLIFE 1 & 2**, **RESTAURANTS 1, 2, 3**, **WINE TAVERNS**.

Nymphenburg: See BUILDINGS 1, NYMPHENBURG, Schloss Nymphenburg.

Oberammergau: See EXCURSION 2.

Odeonsplatz: The square was laid out at the beginning of the 19thC at the behest of the later king Ludwig I. The Hofgarten gate on the east side was built in 1818 and, opposite, Klenze put up residences and offices for the nobility on either side of Brienner Strasse. The Odeon (1828), to which the square owes its name, was originally a ballroom and concert hall famous for its acoustics but it has since been reconstructed as the Ministry of the Interior. The Leuchtenberg-Palais next door was modelled on the Palazzo Farnese in Rome and is now the Ministry of Finance. At the centre of the square stands a statue of King Ludwig I on horseback by Schwanthaler and Widmann (1862). In 1923 a Nazi party rally ended abruptly at the Odeonsplatz with 16 deaths and Hitler's arrest. U-Bahn 3-6 Odeonsplatz. See **WALK 3**.

Oktoberfest: The largest public festival in the world, dating from 1810 when the wedding of Crown Prince Ludwig to Therese von Sachsen-Hildburghhausen was celebrated with a horse race on the meadow now called the Theresienwiese. The modern Oktoberfest is a vast fair with beer tents from all the Munich breweries. It attracts seven million visitors who consume five million litres of beer and 700,000 grilled chickens. On the first day is the procession of horse-drawn brewers' drays to the Wies'n, on the second a procession of bands and folklore groups from all over Europe. See **Events**.

Olympiapark: The former site of Munich's first airport was transformed into a sports and recreational centre when Munich was chosen to host the 1972 Olympic Games. The 60-m-high Olympiaberg was constructed from wartime rubble and the park's lakes were created by damming the Nymphenburg Canal. A futuristic plexiglass 'tent' spreads over the Olympic Hall, stadium (0830-1800; DM 1) and swimming pool (see **Sports**). Towering over all is the 290-m-high Olympiaturm, a good spot from which to view the Alps in clear weather as there are platforms at 189 m and 192 m, as well as an expensive revolving restaurant at 182 m (0800-2230 summer, 0900-2230 winter; DM 4). There are tours of the park at 1100, 1300, 1500 and 1700 (DM 6 including tower, film, brochure). U-Bahn 2, 3 Petuelring.

Opening Times:
Banks – 0830-1230, 1330-1530 Mon.-Fri. (till 1730 Thu.). Major branches do not close at lunchtime.
Post Offices – 0800-1800 Mon.-Fri., 0800-1200 Sat.
Shops – 0900-1830 Mon.- Fri., 0900-1400 Sat. (all day on the first Sat. of the month). Many stay open till 2030 Thu.

Palais Neuhaus-Preysing: See WALK 3.

Palais Törring-Jettenbach: Built in the mid-18thC by the Gunetzrhainer brothers, the palace was rebuilt as the Main Post Office in 1834 when the north facade was redesigned as an open hall of pillars in Florentine style by Leo von Klenze. See BUILDINGS 1, WALK 3.

Paläontologisches Museum: The State Collection of Palaeontology and Historical Geology at Richard-Wagner Strasse 10 contains displays of prehistoric saurians and mammals, plant fossils and finds from southern Germany. There are special exhibitions and monthly slide shows. Open 0800-1600 Mon.-Thu., 0800-1500 Fri., closed hol. U-Bahn 2 Königsplatz.

Parking: The number of cars in Munich has increased enormously in the last few years, resulting in the devising of more one-way systems to keep cars out of the city centre. This has made parking even more difficult and the multi-storey car parks in town quickly fill up. Fines for illegal parking range from DM 5 to at least DM 140 if you are towed away (there are no wheel clamps yet!). A better option than driving is to use the excellent public transport system (see **Transport**). See **Driving**.

Passports & Customs: Citizens of EC countries and of the USA need only a valid passport for stays of up to three months.

Peterskirche: Munich's first parish church, with origins dating back beyond the 12thC, was destroyed in a city fire in 1327. The present building dates from 1607-21 but suffered damage in the war. The basilica church, with its lantern dome and projecting spire, was restored in

rococo style in the 18thC. It features stuccowork and frescoes by J. B. Zimmermann. The high altar by Stuber and Egid Quirin Asam (see **A-Z**) has a figure of St. Peter by Grasser (1492). Further features are the rococo choir stalls by Günther and Dietrich, and the Gothic Schrenk altar dating from around 1400. See **CHURCHES, WALK 2, Alte Peter.**

Petrol: Petrol prices are reasonable and you will probably find that JET stations are the cheapest. The lead content in German petrol is quite low, while lead-free petrol (*Bleifrei*) is widely available. There are many 24-hr, self-service filling stations. See **Driving.**

Police: The main police station is at Ettstrasse 2, tel: 2141 and there are numerous smaller stations (*Polizeiwache*) throughout the city. Police officers wear a dark green uniform and are generally friendly and helpful towards tourists. See **Crime & Theft, Emergency Numbers**.

Post Offices: The Hauptpost (Main Post Office) is across from the station at Bahnhofplatz 1 and offers a 24-hr service for letters, parcels, telegrams and telephones. Its public telex and money-changing services operate from 0700 to 2300. There are poste restante facilities (letters should be addressed to Hauptpost lagernd). Other post office branches open 0800-1800 Mon.-Fri., 0800-1200 Sat. You can also buy stamps from newsagents and the vending machines situated near post boxes. A postcard to the UK costs DM 0.60, to the USA DM 1.05. See **Telephones & Telegrams.**

Propyläen: See BUILDINGS 2.

Public Holidays: 1 Jan. (New Year's Day); 6 Jan. (Epiphany); Good
Friday; Easter Monday; 1 May (Labour Day); Ascension Day; Monday
following Whit Sunday; Corpus Christi; 17 June (German Unity Day);
15 Aug. (Assumption); 1 Nov. (All Saints' Day); third Wed. in Nov. (Day
of Prayer and Repentance); 24 Dec. (half day); 25 Dec. (1st Christmas
Day); 26 Dec. (2nd Christmas Day); 31 Dec. (half day).

Rabies: Exists in Germany as it does in other parts of mainland
Europe. As a precaution all animal bites should be seen by a doctor.

Railways: Munich's main railway station, Hauptbahnhof, is centrally
situated and boasts a tourist office and post office as well as the usual
station facilities. German Federal Railways, Deutsche Bundesbahn
(DB), offer a reliable and comprehensive service to and from the city.
You must pay a supplement on the EuroCity (EC) and InterCity (IC) services, and on the long-distance express trains (FD and D) on journeys
under 50 km. DB also operates a bus network (see **Buses**).
The usual discount passes (e.g. Eurail, Interail, Rail Europe Senior) are
recognized alongside DB's own: the Germanrail Tourist Card (DM 270
for nine days and DM 650 for 16 days, and you must show your passport); the Tourenkarten, valid for ten days within a 21-day period (you
must have already travelled at least 250 km on DB); the Taschengeld
Pass (DM 40, allowing half-fare travel for children aged 12-17).
The DB network also includes Munich's suburban electric railway, or
S-Bahn, covering the surrounding region and crossing the city on an
east-west axis. U-Bahn connections can be made at the Hauptbahnhof,
Karlsplatz, Marienplatz and Ostbuhnhof. See **Transport**.

Religious Services: The following services are conducted in
English:
Catholic – Berchmans Kolleg, Jesuit House, Kaulbachstrasse 31a,
tel: 936193. 1030 Sun.
Anglican/Episcopal – Church of the Ascension in the Emmauskirche,
Seybothstrasse 4, tel: 648185. 0800 Sun.

Baptist – International Baptist Church of Munich, Holzstrasse 9,
tel: 6908534. 1245 Sun. Sunday School at 1145.
United Methodist Church – Friedenskirche, Frauenlobstrasse 5,
tel: 3006100. 1130 Sun.
Nondenominational – Munich International Community Church,
Enhuberstrasse 10, tel: 8508617. 1630 Sun.

Residenz: A complex of buildings surrounding six large courtyards,
the most outstanding of which is the Brunnenhof (Fountain Courtyard),
standing on the site of a small 14thC moated castle. It reached its present grand scale over a period of several centuries, resulting in a variety
of architectural styles. The imposing neoclassical south facade, the
Königsbau, forms one side of the Max-Joseph-Platz (see **A–Z**) and was
modelled by Leo von Klenze on a Florentine *palazzo*. The west facade,
the Maximilianischer Trakt, running along the Residenzstrasse is

Renaissance (1611-19) and features a statue
of the Virgin by Hans Krumper. The 19thC
Festsaalbau on the north side facing the
Hofgarten (see **PARKS & GARDENS**, **A–Z**)
contains the Herkulessaal, one of Munich's
main concert halls (see **Music**). On the
east side is the Marstall which today serves
as a theatre. The Residenzmuseum (see
MUSEUMS 2) constitutes all the rooms of the
Residenz that are open to the public. The
main attractions are the Grottenhof (Grotto
Court), an elegant courtyard with a splendid bronze fountain by Gerhard; the
Antiquarium (Hall of Antiquities), a
Renaissance-style library containing busts
of ancient Greek and Roman leaders; the
Kurfürstenzimmer (Electors' Room); the
17th-18thC Far Eastern porcelain collection; the Hofkapelle; the Reiche Kapelle;
and the Silver Rooms. See **BUILDINGS 1**,
WALK 3.

St. Michael's Church: See Michaelskirche.

St. Peter's Church: See Peterskirche.

Sankt-Johann-Nepomuk-Kirche: See Asamkirche.

Schleissheim: 13 km north of Munich, on the east side of the Dachau moor, are the three palaces of Schleissheim. Duke Wilhelm V first built a modest country retreat here in 1597, which his son Maximilian I turned into the Italianate Altes Schloss (Old Palace). Today it houses part of the Bavarian National Museum collection of Christian objects from all over the world (1000-1700 Tue.-Sun.; DM 3, free Sun. & hol.). The Neues Schloss (New Palace) opposite was commissioned by Prince Elector Max II Emanuel on his triumphant return after defeating the Turks in 1688. The splendid baroque building was begun by Enrico Zuccalli and completed in 1719-27 by Joseph Effner (see **A-Z**). The gold and white facade, in five sections, is 335 m long. Highlights of the rococo interior include fine stuccowork and frescoes, many of which illustrate Max Emanuel's victories. It was here that he also founded one of the first art galleries in Europe, with a collection of around 1000, mainly baroque, paintings (1000-1230, 1330-1600 Tue.-Sun.; DM 2, or DM 3 including admission to Lustheim). At the far end of the beautiful formal park stands the Palace of Lustheim, the charming Italianate residence Max I Emanuel built for his bride. It houses a collection of 18thC Meissen porcelain.

Schliersee: A picturesque town set in beautiful countryside which offers hiking in summer and skiing in winter. The baroque parish church has a light, attractive interior with ceiling paintings and stuccowork by J. B. Zimmermann. The statue of the patron saint of the church, St. Sixtus, dates from 1520 and the group entitled *The Throne of Grace* is attributed to Erasmus Grasser (1480). The painting of the *Virgin in a Mantle* is by Jan Polack (1494).

Schloss Blutenburg: The castle is situated on an island between two arms of the River Würm, an ideal setting for a hunting palace and used as such between 1425 and 1613. The late-Gothic chapel to the right of the entrance houses a winged altarpiece decorated by Jan Polack and wooden statues of Mary (the famous *Blutenburg Madonna*) and the twelve apostles. The inner courtyard features four towers. The castle houses the International Youth Library, and the children's lending library on the left of the outer courtyard has a hall on the floor above for exhibitions and concerts. See **BUILDINGS 1**.

Schloss Linderhof: King Ludwig II's first and favourite castle, the only one he ever saw completed (1874-79), is a homogeneous blend of rococo and baroque styles. Like the palace on which it is loosely modelled, the Petit Trianon of the 'Sun King' Louis XIV, it is lavishly decorated. The building is set in an extensive park with pools, fountains, terraced gardens, a Moorish pavilion and a grotto inspired by the Venusberg of Wagner's opera *Tannhäuser*. See **EXCURSION 2**.

Schloss Lustheim: See **Schleissheim**.

Schloss Nymphenburg: The splendid summer palace of the Bavarian royal family was built for Henriette Adelaide by her husband after she gave birth to their son and heir, Max Emanuel, who added the four pavilions and was strongly influenced by the Palace of Versailles. The high middle section predates his reign and is the oldest part; the semicircle of outbuildings was completed by his successors. The beautiful banqueting hall, the Steinerner Saal, with its music gallery was added in the 1750s. Its frescoes and stuccowork date from the same period and are by J. B. Zimmermann and his son. The rooms in the north wing are in the French style and feature painted panels, carved woodwork and Brussels tapestries. The south wing possesses the Chinese Cabinet reconstructed by Cuvilliés (see **A-Z**) and Ludwig I's famous Gallery of Beauties. Four rooms in the south wing house the Marstallmuseum, a splendid array of ceremonial coaches, harnesses and drawings of Ludwig II's favourite horses. On the first floor is the Nymphenburger Porzellan-Sammlung Bauml with exhibits tracing the manufacture of porcelain at Nymphenburg from 1747 to the 1920s (0900-1230, 1330-1700 Tue.-Sun. summer; 1000-1230, 1330-1600

winter; DM 2). See **BUILDINGS 1**,
NYMPHENBURG.

Schwabing: This district just
north of the Siegestor (see **A-Z**)
began as a village outside the city
boundaries and was not incorporated into the city until the late 19thC.
It became known as Munich's
Bohemian quarter, the haunt of
artists, writers, musicians and actors,
and today is one of the trendiest and
most expensive areas to live in the
city. U-Bahn 3, 6 Münchener
Freiheit.

Sendlinger Tor: See **WALK 1**, City
Fortifications.

Shopping: Munich is an excellent
city for shopping. The best area is
the pedestrian zone stretching from
the Stachus (Karlsplatz – see **A-Z**) to
the Marienplatz (see **A-Z**). The most elegant shops are to be found
along Maximilianstrasse, Theatiner Strasse and Brienner Strasse, while
antique shops are concentrated around the Stachus and the Residenz
(see **BUILDINGS 1**, **WALK 3**, **A-Z**). A visit to the Viktualienmarkt, Munich's
biggest and liveliest fruit and vegetable market, is a must. See **SHOPPING
1, 2, 3**, **Best Buys**, **Opening Times**.

Siegestor (Victory Gate): This copy of the Roman Arch of
Constantine in Ludwigstrasse/Leopoldstrasse was commissioned by
Ludwig I (1843-52) in honour of the Bavarian army and marks the
southern limit of Schwabing (see **A-Z**). U-Bahn 3, 6 Universität.

Siemens-Museum: This collection at Prannerstrasse 10 traces the history of electrotechnology and electronics since the famous firm was founded in 1847 (0900-1600 Mon.-Fri., 1000-1400 Sat., Sun.; free). U-Bahn 3-6 Odeonsplatz; S-Bahn Karlsplatz.

Smoking: Smoking is prohibited in cinema and theatre auditoria, and in the U-Bahn. There are also a few restaurants with no-smoking areas. Although the anti-tobacco campaign has not gained ground as quickly here as in Britain, there is a definite move in that direction.

Sports: The sports shops Sport-Scheck (see **SHOPPING 2**) and Schuster Sport, Rosenstrasse 3-6 organize tennis and sailing courses.
Golf – Nine-hole course at Thalkirchen, tel: 7231304, 18-hole course at Strasslach near Grünwald, tel: 08170450. You can only play during the week if you are a member of a club at home (DM 57).
Tennis – A complete list of courts can be found in the *Yellow Pages* under *Tennisplatzvermietung.* You must book up at least a week in advance. Prices vary according to the day of the week and the time of day (2300-2400 under DM 24, weekend peak time around DM 50).
Sailing – Starnberg and Ammersee are the nearest places where you can sail. Contact the Bayerischer Segler-Verband, Augestenstrasse 46, tel: 5244 for further details.
Mountain walking – A brochure entitled *Bergwandern leicht gemacht* containing details of tours with special ticket offers (June-Oct.) is issued by the German Federal Railways (see **Railways**).
Swimming – Olympia-Schwimmhalle (indoor), Olympiapark (see **A-Z**); Ungererbad (outdoor), Traubestrasse 3. Cost about DM 3.
Ice-skating – Olympiapark (see **A-Z**), Spiridon-Louis Ring 3 (DM 3); in winter on the Kleinhesseloher See, Englischer Garten (see **PARKS & GARDENS**, **A-Z**).

Staatliche Antikensammlung: Neoclassical building containing a Greek-vase collection bettered only by the Louvre's and British Museum's. Many exhibits were collected by Ludwig I. See **MUSEUMS 2**.

Staatliche Graphische Sammlung: This interesting collection at Meiserstrasse 10 comprises sketches and printed graphics from the

15thC to the present day, including works by Dürer and Rembrandt, and romantic and expressionist artists. Open 1000-1300, 1400-1630 Mon.-Wed. (until 1600 Thu., 1300 Fri.); free. U-Bahn 2 Königsplatz; tram 18. See **WALK 3**.

Staatliches Museum für Völkerkunde: The State Ethnological Museum at Maximilianstrasse 42 began life as a collection of curios amassed by the Wittelsbachs in the 16thC. It includes objects from James Cook's travels and the famous Brazilian collection of Munich scientists Spix and Martius. Continued acquisition has brought interesting exhibits from outside Europe, especially Asia, and Central and South America (0900-1630 Tue.-Sun.; DM 5). Tram 19, 20. See **WALK 2**.

Staatsgalerie Moderner Kunst: See **MUSEUMS 1**.

Stachus: See **Karlsplatz**.

Statue of Bavaria: This giant bronze figure symbolizing Bavaria, stands in the Theresienwiese, site of the Oktoberfest, and was unveiled during the 1850 festivities. Climb the 126 steps for a stunning view of the city (1000-1200, 1400-1730 Tue.-Sun., Oktoberfest 1000-2000 Mon.-Sun.). U-Bahn 4, 5 Messegelände; bus 31, 32.

Straub, Johann Baptist (1704-84): Appointed as Munich's Court Sculptor in 1737, Straub went on to execute many fine pieces throughout the city and surrounding area. You can see some of his works at Schloss Nymphenburg (see **BUILDINGS 1, NYMPHENBURG, A-Z**), Ettal (see **EXCURSION 2, A-Z**) and the Altes Residenztheater (see **A-Z**).

Taxis: Munich taxis are plentiful, but rather expensive (DM 3.30 pick-up charge and DM 1.90 per km thereafter, extra DM 1 for phone reservation). You can hail one in the street, catch one at a rank or reserve one by phone, tel: 21610. See **Tipping, Transport**.

Tegernsee: The former monastery of Tegernsee (also comprising a church, palace, grammar school and brewery) was founded in AD 719 and for centuries was a cultural centre for Bavaria and a source of literary works. The monastery church of St. Quirin, originally Romanesque, combines a variety of architectural styles. The facade was remodelled in 1824 in imitation of Santa Trinita dei Monti in Rome, but the twin towers date back to the 11thC. It contains sculptures by Johann Baptist Straub (see **A-Z**) and frescoes by Hans Georg Asam.

Telephones & Telegrams: The telephone service is operated by the Post Office. Phone boxes are yellow. A local call will cost DM 0.30 and you will need 10 Pf and DM 1 and 5 coins (cheap rate 1800-0800). International and long-distance calls can be made from boxes bearing a green sign marked *Inlands- und Auslandsgespräche*.

Directory Enquiries	1188
International Enquiries	00118
Local Operator	010
International Operator	0010

Telegrams can be sent by phone, tel: 1131, or from any post office.

Television & Radio: AFN (American Forces Network) radio can be picked up in Munich as can AFN TV in those areas of the city which lie close to the forces' base. There are two English-language cable TV channels, Super Channel and Eurosport.

Theatinerkirche: See CHURCHES.

Time Difference: One hour ahead of GMT. Clocks go forward one hour in summer, so the time difference is always maintained.

Tipping: In general, waiters and taxi drivers expect to 'keep the change' – usually up to 10% of the bill or fare. Give porters DM 1-2 per item of luggage and hairdressers and guides a 10-15% tip.

Tourist Information: The central tourist office (*Fremdenverkehrsamt*) is at Sendlingerstrasse 1 near Marienplatz (see **A-Z**), tel: 23911 (0800-1500 Mon.-Thu., 0830-1400 Fri.). There is also a branch inside the Hauptbahnhof (see **Railways**) at the Bayerstrasse exit,

tel: 2391256 (0800-2300). For the office at the airport (see **A-Z**), tel: 907256 (0830-2200 Mon.-Sat., 1300-2100 Sun. & hol.). Finally, there is another branch at the Neues Rathaus (see **A-Z**) which is open 0900-1700 Mon.-Thu., 0900-1630 Fri. Call 239163 for recorded information on museums and galleries, 239173 for palaces and other monuments, 239181 for exhibitions and fairs. Information on Upper Bavaria can be obtained from Fremdenverkehrsverband München-Oberbayern, Sonnenstrasse 10/-III, D-8000 Munich 2, tel: 597347. See **Accommodation**, **Tours**, **What's On**.

Tours: Münchener Fremden-Rundfahrten OHG, Hauptbahnhof, Arnulfstrasse 8, tel: 591504, organize city tours (1000 & 1430 daily; DM 13 for 1 hr, DM 20-23 for 2 hr 30 min). Their buses leave from the Bahnhofplatz opposite the main entrance to the station. The Munich Volkshochschule, tel: 480060, offers weekly guided walking tours around the city (May-Oct.; DM 6 for around 2 hr).

Transport: Munich has an efficient, integrated public-transport system, Münchner Verkehrs- und Tarifverbund, or MVV, consisting of bus and tram services, the S-Bahn (suburban railway) and U-Bahn (underground). The fares structure operates on a zone system and zone maps are displayed in all stations and at bus and tram stops. The system runs from about 0500-0100 and one ticket is valid on any form of transport. Zones are coded blue for the inner city and green for outlying areas covered by the S-Bahn. You must always stamp your ticket in the validating machines on buses, trams and at the entrances to U-Bahn and S-Bahn stations. Checks by inspectors are regular and those travelling without a valid stamped ticket will incur a hefty, on-the-spot fine.

You can buy a ticket entitling you to 24-hr unlimited travel from blue vending machines at S-Bahn and U-Bahn stations, kiosks displaying a white K and at tourist offices (see **Tourist Information**), and this is probably the simplest option if you plan to travel about during the day. These cost DM 7.50 for the blue zone only, and DM 15 for both green and blue zones (DM 2.50 & DM 4.50 respectively for children aged 4-14). There are also strip tickets available from blue vending machines, places displaying a white K and on buses. A blue strip ticket with 16 strips costs DM 15; two strips are valid for up to two hours, you can break your journey but must not change direction. Single tickets cost DM 2.40 within Munich or DM 1.30 for a 'short trip' (i.e. two U- or S-Bahn stops or four bus or tram stops) and can be used in green and blue zones. A trip in the inner-city blue zone is two strips, or one for a 'short trip'. Otherwise, stamp two strips in the machine per green zone travelled in. See **Buses**, **Driving**, **Railways**, **Taxis**, **U-Bahn**.

Traveller's Cheques: See **Money**.

U-Bahn: The U-Bahn (underground) network covers areas in many parts of the city and is presently being extended. Connections to the S-Bahn network exist at the Hauptbahnhof, Karlsplatz, Marienplatz and Ostbahnhof (see **Railways**). The system is an excellent one with frequent trains. Services run 0500-0100 Sun.-Thu., 0500-0200 Fri.-Sat. See **Transport**.

Universität: Originally founded in 1472 by Duke Ludwig the Rich in Ingolstadt, the university was not introduced to Munich until

1826 by Ludwig I. A new home was created for it by Gärtner in 1835-40 on Geschwister-Scholl-Platz. Set amid lawns on each side of the Ludwigstrasse, the two fountains modelled on those in St. Peter's Sq. in Rome add an elegant finishing touch. U-Bahn 3, 6 Universität.

Valentin-Musäum: Offbeat collection of absurdities in memory of the great Munich comedian Karl Valentin (1882-1948). Exhibits in the second tower illustrate the history of old Munich folk singers in documents and pictures. Open 1101-1729 Mon., Tue., Sat., 1001-1729 Sun. S-Bahn Isartor; tram 18, 20. See **WALK 2**.

What's On: The official *Monatsprogram* (*Monthly Programme*), issued by the tourist office, is available at kiosks, newsagents and in some bookshops (DM 1.80). However, those who don't read German can buy the English-language magazine *Munich Found* at the Internationale Presse in the Hauptbahnhof (see **Railways**) or at the Anglia Bookshop, Scellingstrasse 3 (DM 2.50). Up-to-date information for students is contained in the *Young People's Guide to Munich* which can be obtained from the Hauptbahnhof tourist office (see **Tourist Information**). See **Events**, **Newspapers**.

Wieskirche (Meadow Church): One of the finest rococo churches in Germany was built by Dominikus and Johann Baptist Zimmermann between 1746-54 to accommodate a miraculous wooden figure of the *Scourged Redeemer*. The whitewashed walls and plain-glass windows of the interior give an overall impression of light and harmony. The ceiling is decorated with a huge fresco of the *Judgement Day*, while statues of the four Church Fathers stand in the nave. The choir is richly furnished with columns, balustrades, statues, gilt stuccowork and frescoes. See **EXCURSION 2**.

Wittelsbacher Brunnen: Munich's most attractive fountain, situated in the centre of Lenbachplatz, is the work of Adolf von Hildebrand (1883-85) and features the figures of a woman sitting on a bull, symbol-

izing the beneficial power of water, and a boy on horseback, symbolizing its destructive power. U-Bahn 4, 5; S-Bahn Karlsplatz. See **WALK 3**.

Youth Hostels:
DJH Jugendherberge – Wendl-Dietrich-Strasse 20, 8 Munich 19, tel: 131156.
DJH Jugendgästehaus Thalkirchen – Miesingstrasse 4, 8 Munich 70, tel: 7236550.
Prices for bed and breakfast start at about DM 18.
To stay in one of these hostels you must be under 28 years old and have a youth hostel identification card. These can be purchased at the youth hostels themselves or the Youth Information Centre, Paul-Heyse-Strasse 22 (1100-1900 Mon.-Fri., 1100-1700 Sat; DM 30), but it is cheaper to buy one in the UK before you arrive.
There are also slightly more expensive youth hotels which cost from DM 25 for a dormitory bed (details from the tourist office – see **Tourist Information** – or the Youth Information Centre). There is a CVJM (YMCA) at Landwehrstrasse 13, tel: 555941.